Saving Christian Marriage

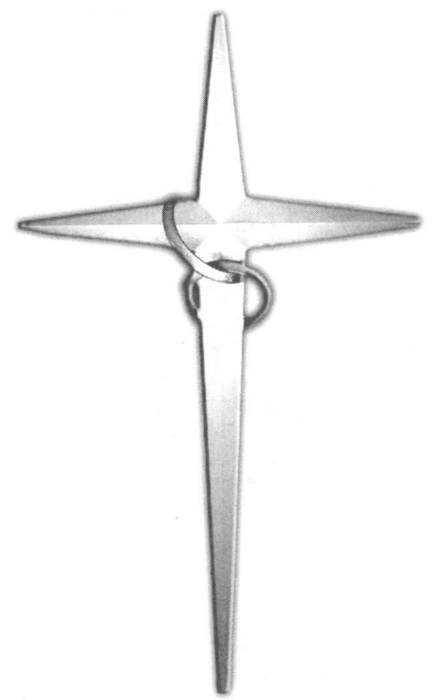

The Wanderer Forum Foundation

TABLE OF CONTENTS

Office of the Bishop

Diocese of Rockford
555 Colman Center Drive
P.O. Box 7044
Rockford, Illinois 61125

This set of essays in the <u>Wanderer</u> <u>Forum</u> <u>Foundation</u> is valuable even though some of the individual contributions go back some three decades.

As we are always grateful to Almighty God, we know that some aspects of our Catholic doctrine do not change despite the velleities of *quidnuncs* and the unwary.

One who reads them in the context in which they were written can easily apply their sound and prudent teaching to the circumstances of our day. I commend the writers of the individual pieces and the <u>Wanderer</u> <u>Forum</u> <u>Foundation</u> for putting together this useful booklet.

With every good wish, I remain

Cordially yours in Christ,

+ Thomas G. Doran

The Most Reverend Thomas G. Doran, D.D., J.C.D.
Bishop of Rockford

Preface

When the first National Wanderer Forum was held in 1965, the Second Vatican Council was ending and the cultural revolution of the 1960s was moving into high gear. Over the next three decades, national and regional Wanderer Forums analyzed the teaching of the Church on many issues, including the liturgy, national defense, the rights of workers, and, of course, the life and family issues which are the focus of this present volume, aptly titled, *Saving Christian Marriage.*

"A family policy," said John Paul II, "must be the basis and the driving force of all social policies" (*Evangelium Vitae*, n. 90). This is so because the family is "the basic cell of society" (*Letter to Families*, n. 4). Civil society depends on the family for its very future. To put it simply, only the union of a man and woman can produce new taxpayers. The more important point, however, is that the "model of the family," in the words of John Paul, is "in God Himself, in the Trinitarian mystery of His life" (*Letter to Families*, n. 6). That mystery is one of communion among the divine persons. Similarly, the "covenant of marriage...opens the spouses to a lasting communion of love and of life, and it is brought to completion...with the procreation of children. The communion of the spouses gives rise to this community of the family" (Pope John Paul II, *Letter to Families*, n. 7).

For the past three centuries, the philosophers and politicians of the Enlightenment have sought to build a society as if God did not exist. The main target of their attack is the family. The Enlightenment premises are secularism (there is no God), relativism (there is no objective moral truth) and individualism (I am my own god and can make up my own moral rules). The answer to those premises and the way to victory over those attacks, especially those against life and the family, will be found only in the social and moral teachings of the Catholic Church. Those teachings do not change and they are true. The sole purpose of the Wanderer Forum has been and continues to be to promote those teachings. That is why we offer in this book a collection of incisive essays that will make those teachings come alive.

This little book presents ten pertinent commentaries on Christian Marriage, eight of which are addresses from the Ninth National Wanderer Forum in 1973, shortly after the U.S. Supreme Court decision in *Roe v Wade* legalized the execution of unborn babies. Those addresses offer analyses that will be helpful to the reader today, especially with respect to the decisive impact of contraception on every aspect of the present crisis of marriage and the family. The speakers do not sugar-coat the reality that we are in a cultural and religious war. Nor do they mince words about the defeats we have suffered because of the timidity and even treason of some of our leaders, clerical as well as lay. In addition, two contemporary authors have added their observations on more recent developments in the continuing assaults on marriage.

This, however, is not a pessimistic book. One cannot read these addresses without drawing from the wellspring of the great spirituality the Church has to offer on this topic. The words of many of these knowing authors have to do with grace, salvation, and a clear focus on God – something so desperately needed today and so obviously missing in many forms of catechesis and instruction for both young and old alike. Reading these words from the past is not a trip of nostalgia, but the realization that they were voices crying in the wilderness, warning us of things to come and presenting a clear picture of the safe path of sanctity to be taken through the coming morass.

"The Church is alive," said Pope Benedict XVI at the Mass for the Inauguration of his Pontificate. "And the Church is young. She holds within herself the future of the world and therefore shows each of us the way towards the future." These words surely encompass the wisdom found in the pages of this book, *Saving Christian Marriage.*

–Charles E. Rice, Chairman
Wanderer Forum Foundation

The Splendor
of the
Christian Marriage

Most Rev. Godfrey M. P. Okoye
Bishop of Enugu, Nigeria

Present-day Catholic theology of marriage is opposed by powerful influences attempting to interpret marriage and family life as purely profane and earthly realities. Vast masses of people and unfortunately of the baptized and not only people of weak will but even morally mature men and women let themselves be tainted, without noticing it, by a secularist view of marriage that is full of strange and extravagantly false ideas that are served up in newspapers, magazines, films, and television as objective truths about married life.

"The enemy of our salvation (*I Pt.* 5:8ff) today persuades men with greater insistence and cunning. We are all aware of the increasing rate of divorce. We are aware of the insistence with which certain means of propaganda promote practices which offend against conjugal chastity. Vicious propaganda is relentlessly pushing forward the cult of pleasure without any regard to the true nature and splendor and holy ideal of conjugal intimacy.

"Furthermore, conscientious parents lament certain conditions which today militate against that training of their children which will make them mature, responsible and holy citizens."[1]

Anybody who has not been struck blind can see the devastation that these ideas have wrought within the sanctuary of the family and how chaotic their consequences are and will continue to be in human society.

Marital discord and infidelity, broken families, and the poverty of the joy and piety that should characterize our Christian families are a challenge to Christians and theologians and pastors, and force them to reflect deeply on the religious nature and splendor of Christian marriage and family life.

Marriage as A Sacred Reality and Divine Institution

It is the Second Vatican Council that has in a most special way re-emphasized what had already existed in the teaching of the Popes;[2] namely, that to understand and appreciate all the real beauty and grandeur of marriage, we must strive to see it through the eyes of Christ; to see it from His own point of view, in its relationship to God. We must, therefore, strive to acquire Christ's attitude and outlook towards marriage. Through Christ every intimate detail of married life assumes all the joy and happiness and fullness of life intended for this sacred state.

Marriage belongs completely to God. It is something entirely in His hands. He instituted it. Once we understand this, we possess the first essential fact to be realized concerning the nature of marriage. That marriage is a Divine institution is aptly summarized in this short prayer uttered by young Tobias:

"Thou madest Adam, and gavest him Eve his wife for a helper and stay: of them came mankind: Thou hast said, It is not good that man should be alone; let us make unto him an aid like unto himself. And now, O Lord, I take not this my sister for lust but uprightly: therefore mercifully ordain that we may become aged together. And she said with him, Amen." (*Tobit.* 8:6-9).

Marriage Is A Vocation

If marriage is a Divine institution, those who embrace the married state should realize that it is a response to a Divine call. Married people are invited by God to embrace this way of life as the state in which they are to mold their life and character and become living replicas of Christ and thus be assured of their eternal happiness.

Christian marriage, therefore, is not something to be looked down upon as a concession to those who are not called to the dignity of the priesthood or of the Religious life. It is not something merely tolerated or permitted. This was the puritanistic anti-sex and anti-marriage view expressed by the Manicheans.

Marriage is a call. How does God give this call? Not exactly like the call to the priesthood or the religious life. To put it simply, God intends marriage as the usual way of life — as a state for the sanctification and salvation of the married couples. In married life sanctification will be gained through the union of the husband and wife, a union in which there must be complete submission by both parties to the conditions of marriage as established by God.

To appreciate the full scope of the splendor of Christian marriage in the Divine plan we must go to the Scripture. Here we find that God created woman to be a helpmate for man, "a help mate for him " (*Gen.* 2:18). Helpmate! Companion! Hers, of course is to be no mere status of some sort of assistant-reproducer with no further nor higher purpose in life. God's aim in creating the woman is not merely for the gift of herself to her husband in the short-lived act of procreation. To restrict her value in such a way would be to lower her worth to a point comparable to that of a mere animal in the mating process. Her rightful status is shown by these Scriptural words, "A man shall leave his father and mother and cleave to his wife, and they shall be two in one flesh."

They will be two beings united, each giving to the other constant, undivided love, each complementing the other, finding ever increasing joy and fulfillment in their union together as day by day they mould their life to reflect ever more clearly and perfectly the image of Christ Who dwells in their hearts and home. This is the meaning of their call and in this lies the splendor of Christian married life.

Sacramentality of Christian Marriage[3]

Nowhere does the grandeur and beauty and salvific power of Christian marriage shine out as in its sacramentality. As a natural contract, marriage is the act of mutual consent by which a man and woman give to each other the right to relations and to the normal features of married life: living together and cooperating to meet their common needs and interests. In the Old Law, this natural contract was incapable of giving grace even though it belonged entirely to God.

When, however, Christ came on Earth, He lifted this natural contract into one of His abiding saving mysteries. Christ the Lord is the wellspring of grace. "Of His fullness we have all received" (*John* 1:16). Through His Life, Death, and Resurrection, He has made all things new (*Apoc.* 21:15), healed them, and conferred on them a new holiness. He has thus abundantly blessed marriage and conferred on it a new holiness.[4]

Through Christ this supremely natural reality became a supremely supernatural reality fitted to the task laid on it of revealing the dimensions of the mystery of salvation.

In making marriage a Sacrament, Christ simply took the natural contract and made the Sacrament identical with it. Henceforth, the very act of mutual consent by which a Christian man and woman become husband and wife is capable of giving them grace. Every Sacrament is an encounter with Christ. As the marrying pair meet each other in their consent, they meet Christ as well who now makes perceptible and active in them His saving effectiveness. Christ becomes sovereignly effective to bind and sanctify these two people. The partners themselves achieve in this Sacrament a veiled contact with the Lord. This is what it means to say that marriage is a Sacrament.

Marriage as a Saving Mystery

From the sacramentality of marriage flows its salvific value. In the sacred ceremony of this Sacrament, the bridal pair themselves are the chosen tools of Christ's sanctifying and saving work. As they give the consent of marriage with sincere hearts they open for themselves the treasury of sacramental grace, from which they can draw supernatural strength that will enable them to fulfill their obligations and functions faithfully, holily, and perseveringly until death. In the words of Vatican II:

> "The spouses are fortified by grace and receive a kind of consecration in the duties and dignity of their state, so that as they fulfill their conjugal and family obligations, they are penetrated with the spirit of Christ. This spirit suffuses their whole lives with faith, hope, and charity. Thus they increasingly advance their own perfections as well as their mutual sanctification, and hence contribute jointly to the glory of God."[5]

The salvific dimension of the exchange of consent must be very clearly and constantly brought to the forefront in our marriage instructions to prospective couples. The words "I will" with which couples pledge to each other a love ready to carry out God's aim of living in unity and bringing new life into the world, and the continual discharging of this promise, have a bearing on their salvation.

From the altar, the married couple, therefore, take away with them a binding and honorable pastoral task. It is they who by the love of Christ and the Church have brought the Sacrament to each other and it is they who in the first instance have the care of each other's souls.

When St. Paul said, "…The husband is the head of the wife, as Christ is the head of the Church" (*Eph.* 5:23), his first and principal purpose should be understood as a religious one. It means that a man must lead his wife and children in the witness of faith, in trust in God, in steadfast love and in the working of God. Only then does he become like Christ, Who is "the savior of His body" — the Church (*Eph.* 5:23).

Likewise the wife should so behave in the family and should so honor her husband that she gives him a better idea of his true dignity. She should so turn the various affairs of everyday life in the family into a manifestation of married love that she will thereby fulfill her responsibility for the salvation of her husband. "Likewise, ye wives, be in subjection to your own husbands; that, if any obey not the word, they also may without the word be won by the conversation of the wives; While they behold your chaste conversation" (*I Pt.* 3:1-2), and by the way their wives behave.

Christian Marriage:
An Image of the Love Between Christ and the Church

In one of the prayers in the *New Rite of Marriage* the Church thus prays for the married couple, "Father, in the fulfillment of this Sacrament, the marriage of Christian man and woman is a sign of the marriage between Christ and the Church." And in another prayer we read, "Father, You have made the union of man and wife so holy a mystery that it symbolizes the marriage of Christ and His Church."

In the Christian tradition beginning with St. Paul, Christian marriage has always been regarded as being a profound spiritual reality modelled upon the union of Christ with His Church. In order to grasp a little of the beauty and splendor that is Christian marriage, we must, therefore, understand better the deep mystery of the union of Christ with the Church, and see therein the perfect love which should be typical of the two in one flesh in Christian marriage.

Christ came on Earth only for His Church, the society that He wished to found. As soon as founded, the Church's only concern henceforth was for Christ, her Master: Christ gives Himself entirely and dies for the Church. The Church suffers and is persecuted constantly as she struggles to win more souls for Christ, souls in which and through which Christ continues to live on Earth in His Church.

A union as intimate, a fusion of hearts as complete, an affection as mutual, exclusive, and durable as that of Christ for His Church and the Church's for Christ is the model God intended for marriage when He raised it to the dignity of a Sacrament. Any Christian marriage that falls short of this ideal will flounder helplessly around in the midst of unending confusion and frustration. On the other hand, the Christian couple's faith in this mystery of the mutual love between Christ and the Church, to which it is their task to bear witness, enables them to persevere together even in times of suffering and to look forward in trust to the second coming of Christ when all the love between Christ and His Church and all love sanctified in Christ, will be brought to a glorious consummation.

Factors That Jeopardize The Splendor of Married Life

The Church in her moral teaching remains ever loyal to the authentic principles but realizes as well the struggle required for the attainment of the ideal. The Christian in this world is an ever perfectible being. He is often beset with difficulties.

In the field of married life the Christian today is beset with difficulties in the attainment of the ideal. His married life is often placed in jeopardy by forces both within and outside himself. It is for this reason that we shall not simply stop at outlining the holy ideal of Christian marriage as intended by God and sanctified by Christ, but must also touch, even if briefly, the problems our married couples face in today's world and suggest practical helps towards the overcoming of these problems.

Most conspicuous among these problems are: lack of true love, marital infidelity, and false notions and practices of responsible parenthood. Let us consider them briefly and singly:

Lack of True Love

Love is the mainstay of married life. Where there is no love there will be no successful marriage. Many think and say they love, but love is often not well understood. In the words of Jean Guitton:

> "Like every reality in creation love is composed of
> two elements which in fact are indivisible, but, by right,
> supremely distinct, one of which, at least if love develops
> in an ordered fashion, is subordinate to the other. The
> one derives from the body and animality, the other from
> freedom and the spirit."[6]

When we speak of love being the mainstay of marriage we should understand principally spiritual love, true Christian love, the love born of God which guides all loves.

But what do we often see but the contrary. In fact when people today speak of love they are referring to no other love but the instinctive and erotic love which without the *agape* is in constant danger of imbalance. This type of love is superficially more attractive and vastly easier to follow. It is the type of love that leads to so many divorces and remarriages in today's society. When people speak of such a love they are not only indulging in fairy tales fit only for the frustrated but they are also giving an utterly erroneous idea of love.

Such a love is often selfish and egoistic and does not know what is sacrifice. Such a passing love cannot stand the test of Christian marriage, since it is often limited to the emotional satisfaction of people's unruly desires.

The Christian love required in marriage is Divine love. It is benevolent and consists mostly in giving and sacrificing. It is solicitous for the happiness and salvation of the loved one. It is this love that transforms and ennobles and guides the married couple in their intimate relationships.

Marital Infidelity

Another danger that threatens the married life today is unfaithfulness in marriage. So many reasons account for that. We have the venomous influence of some advertising agents and exaggerated newspaper reportings. There is so much talk of the "inseparable companion" even among the married people.

While we must rejoice today at the progress in the emancipation of women we must likewise lament the dangers that can confront both men and women today in their places of work. A little disagreement in the family, a discovery of unfaithfulness by one of the spouses, and a thousand and one other things can arise in the family which can be for one of the spouses an occasion for a temptation to which he or she can easily succumb given the circumstances of today's industrialized life.

The long absences and long separation between husbands and wives occasioned by the nature of their work can be very trying to marital fidelity, whilst we do not doubt that for some it may increase the desire to return to their homes.

There is need today more than ever for greater formation of both men and women in the solid Christian virtues especially that of conjugal chastity if they will withstand the dangers to their marital fidelity created by life in the modern world.

The Problem of Family Planning

We must in all sincerity admit that one of the greatest difficulties that face the consciences of our Christians, one that debars a good number from living their Christianity to the full is the question of birth control. Even in Africa where children are greatly desired, this is becoming a problem among the urban middle class.

We shall not go here into details as the problem is already well known to our audience. There is no one here who is ignorant of the extent to which human technology has led people into untold means of birth control all in order to contradict the laws of the Creator. What shall we say of such practices as abortion and infanticide?

The problem that faces the loud clamor for birth control is insincerity. What are we up to? Do we see with the Church? If we do, here is the Church's view: "Conjugal love requires in husband and wife an awareness of their mission of 'responsible parenthood' " (*Humanae Vitae*).

Welcoming children, as understood in Catholic morality in conjunction with a certain planning of births in responsibility before God in accordance with the same Catholic morality is vastly different from its counterpart in birth control which is simply and in an unqualified manner hostile to large numbers of children.

The Church opposes immoral means of birth control because they are immoral and because she is aware of the danger to which universal admission of contraception would lead us. It may be helpful to mention but a few. If marital union is shorn of its procreative purpose, what shall one say of extra-marital relationships or even of flirtations within marriage. If it is all right for man and wife to enjoy themselves while deliberately excluding the begetting of children by artificial contraception, how shall we be able to reprimand unmarried boys and girls if they also have recourse to such means.

Widespread approval and practice of contraception leads to a general lowering of the moral tone of society. Discipline and self-control will give way to license and self-indulgence.

The problem of birth control in short is the problem of sexual control. Birth control, therefore, should be handled hand in hand with the virtue of chastity which teaches us that the sexual urges can be mastered and kept within bounds by Divine love — *agape*.[7]

Realization of the Ideal In Christian Married Life

1. Chaste Courtship

Courtship as a prelude to marriage must be taken seriously like marriage itself. It is an important preparation for marriage and sometimes can be regarded as more important because if there is bad courtship the married life is already jeopardized. There should be holiness in the preparation, in the interpersonal relationship that precedes this holy institution. Chastity in those who are engaged is a prelude to true love in the married life because if there is no reverence before marriage there will be no reverence in married life.

2. Self-Mastery And Self-Denial In Married Life

Nowhere else is the saying of Christ more true, that "whosoever shall seek to save his life shall lose it: and whosoever shall lose it shall preserve it" (*Luke* 17:33) and "He that loveth his life shall lose it and he that hateth his life in this world keepeth it unto life eternal" (*John* 12:25). Since Christian marriage is patterned on the self-sacrificing love of Christ for His Church, Christian couples cannot but follow in the footsteps of Christ, daily taking up their cross and following Jesus (*Luke* 9:23). "They are bound to have such feelings for one another as to cherish always very great mutual love, to be ever faithful to their marriage vow, and to give to one another an unfailing and unselfish help."[8]

Truly, there will be times of joy and ecstasy. But the secret behind any successful marriage will always be sacrifice, self-mastery, and self-denial, rooted in that deep reverence by which one will always study to please and not to hurt the other. It will always be the joy of the spouses to give, rather than to receive (cf. *Acts* 20:35), to be deprived rather than to cause concern, sorrow, or suffering to the other. Christian couples who observe this fundamental rule of the Gospel will experience such a deepening and enrichment of their love that their marriage will grow from strength to strength towards the ideal splendor that God intends for Christian marriage.

3. Large-Heartedness And Forgiveness

Large-heartedness and forgiveness is another virtue that should flourish in an ideal Christian family. Let Christian families ask themselves: "Are we large-hearted enough to let bygones be bygones, to forgive and forget, not to nurse injuries and wrongs, not to study how to hurt the other by words and deed?" Peace and happiness will abound in the family if the man and his wife are ready each time to write off the past and to begin afresh on a clean page.

4. True Spiritual Love

Authentic marital love must thoroughly animate married life if it will not be left to be dominated by a purely sensual element. This love must be the love born of God, the love that guides all loves. It is benevolent love and consists mostly in giving, sacrificing, submission, and solicitude for the happiness, and salvation of the loved one.

This conjugal love overflows towards the offspring and surrounds the children with affection and godly concern, so that confident in the love and affection of their parents, they are brought up mature and responsible citizens, lovers of God, and fellowmen.

Conjugal love expresses itself in the marital union, hence the spouses must be faithful in love to each other so that marital intercourse may express and foster conjugal love and fidelity and also help the practice of chastity in the state of wedlock. Therefore, there should be no excessive preoccupation about sex that can easily deprive them of the joy of mutual love. Balanced love is not overanxious about sex.

5. Married Heroism

The splendor and grandeur of Christian married life and love sometimes demands heroism. Let us listen to Pope Pius XII:

> "Heroism is sometimes called for, whether it be
> to respect the purpose of matrimony willed by God; or
> to resist the ardent and insistent stimulations of passions
> and the solicitations which lure a troubled heart to look

elsewhere for that which it has not found in its lawful marriage or does not believe itself to have found so fully as to repay all it had hoped."

"How many intimate dramas lie hidden behind the veil of daily life! How many hidden heroic sacrifices! How many anxieties of the spirit in order that married couples may live together and remain constant in a Christian way to their own place of duty" (*To the Newlyweds*, August 20th, 1941).

The case of a childless marriage is also a case that calls for heroism on the part of the couple so affected. It is a great sorrow for them to find themselves childless. This is even more true in my country than in yours. Their difficult position is understandable, but here again, as I said before, is a case for heroism in marriage. It demands great faith to preserve fidelity. But if after all human and licit means have been tried and yet there is no offspring, Christian couples have the grace to accept God's will.

Great rewards await those who endure such crucial trials for the love of God. They carry a heavy cross for Christ and for the love of Christ. Therefore, great indeed will be their reward in the Kingdom of Christ. They have borne witness to Him. They have confessed Him before men, they have shown their determination to cling to Him at all costs. He will also confess them before His Father in Heaven and will reward them most abundantly by granting them the joy of His company forever.

Conclusion

My wish and hope is that all may respect the sanctity and holiness of marriage so that its splendor may shine out more brightly. Every vocation in life has its difficulties and demands sacrifice. The state of wedlock is no exception. Created in a certain order which was destroyed by sin, this union is recreated in Christ at a level of perfection which it could only attain with the help of redemptive grace. It is this grace which will restore for married couples the wounded human unity, not in a perfect sense, since there may still be lapses, but nonetheless in a real sense, because they have sacramentally been joined to God.

The husband and wife who give the consent of marriage with sincere hearts open for themselves the treasury of sacramental grace, from which they can draw supernatural strength, enabling them to fulfill their obligations and functions faithfully, holily, and perseveringly until death. By sacramental marriage, Christian couples obtain a right to the help of whatever grace they need for the discharge of their matrimonial duties (*Casti Connubii*, Pius XI).

On our part as pastors we must not indulge in exaggerated pessimism. In every Christian the sense of growth to perfection is already evident from the day of his baptism. There are well-intentioned couples who are determined to live up to the standard and who are actually doing so. We must not allow the aberrations in the married life of the noisy minority to overshadow the great efforts of the silent majority. What we hear and see in newspapers should not blind us to the enduring value and sacredness and splendor of Christian marriage.

For the rest, the Church is a teacher as well as a mother. In her teaching and moral demands she remains ever loyal to the authentic principles but adopts equally the pedagogy of patient expectation for the fullness of time, the eschatological time, the final time when all will be perfect, when there will be no more marrying and giving in marriage and when the splendor of married life will give way to the splendor of the beatific vision of Heaven for those who have lived faithful married lives.

ENDNOTES

1.   G.M.P. Okoye, C.S.Sp., *The Sacredness of Marriage and Family Life*, p. 9-11.
2.   Notably: *Arcanum Divinae Sapientiae*, Leo XIII, February 10, 1880; *Casti Connubii*, Pius XI, Dec. 31, 1930; "Allocution to Midwives," Pius XII, October 29, 1951; *Humanae Vitae*, Paul VI, July 25th, 1968.
3.   *The Sacredness of Marriage and Family Life*, G. M. P. Okoye, C.S.Sp. cit., p. 17-23.
4.   *Ibid.*, p. 17.
5.   *The Church in the Modern World*, n. 48
6.   Jean Guitton, *Human Love*, 1966, p. 57. The author is certainly referring here to instinctive and erotic love on the one hand and *agape* of spiritual love on the other.
7.   G.M.P. Okoye, C.S.Sp., *The Sacredness of Marriage and Family Life*, p. 9-11.
8.   *Arcanum Div. Sap.*, Leo XIII.

Bishop Godfrey Mary Paul Okoye, C.S.Sp., delivered the keynote address at the Ninth National Wanderer Forum in 1973. Bishop Okoye was ordained in 1947. He served in many pastoral capacities in Nigeria and served as rector to the seminary. He became Bishop of Port Harcourt in 1961 and Bishop of Enugu in 1970. Bishop Okoye wrote numerous books and founded four religious congregations, including the Daughters of Divine Love. He died in 1977.

THE SPLENDOR OF THE SACRAMENTAL UNION

Msgr. Alphonse Popek
Milwaukee, Wisconsin

Man, whether he plants or leaves the earth fallow, whether he builds or destroys, gathers or scatters, always leaves clues as to his identity. Wittingly or unwittingly he leaves telltale marks which identify him as the responsible agent for his action or inaction. Whether fallen and still unregenerated in nature, or fallen and redeemed by Christ, there is always evidence of his inclination to evil and his falling short of the ideal of holiness. Since this is true in the process of recognizing man for who and what he is, it is the more true in the recognition of God, the Creator of man.

Everywhere in the universe which surrounds this tiny planet man inhabits, there are "fingerprints and footprints" of God's trans-cendent-imminent Presence. These Divine clues lead to the conclusion that all creation, emanating from His thrice-holy Being, is essentially sacramental. The first man was formed out of the dust of the earth into which God breathed His Holy Spirit; He did the same when He created the first woman. By this direct act of creation the progenitors of the entire human race were sacral, for God, after creating all things, paused to say: "Let us make man to our image and likeness."[1] By Divine design, therefore, Adam and Eve, equal but different, were drawn together into that holy state of marriage which is the pattern of all future marriages. God Himself was the witness in Paradise when our first parents freely and mutually entered into that first contract between one man and one woman forming the spiritual and physical relationship which is marriage.

How resplendent marriage is in its sacredness even as a natural contract between man and woman. Marriage, as a Divine invention for man's temporal and eternal blessedness, is essentially sacramental. First of all the sacredness of natural wedlock flows from the historic fact that the all-holy God Himself established marriage as the ordinary means of propagating His choicest creatures. Is it any wonder that, as with Christian and as with pagan, the begetting of children is dignified with the name of "procreation" indicating the unmerited cooperation of human beings in what God had done primevally when He directly created the first man and woman. Secondly, natural wedlock is sacred because it is a means of mutual help for husband and wife not only toward material and temporal progress but toward their only true and eternal destiny – God. Considering man's nature weakened by Original Sin, he – without this holy arrangement – would be no better than the beast of the forest merely exploiting his procreative potential with unbridled passion to his own natural and supernatural destruction, creating a Hell on Earth and preparing himself for a Hell in eternity.

Pope Pius XI declared:

> "…Marriage, before being a union of body, is first and more intimately a union and harmony of minds, brought about not by any passing affection of sense or heart but by a deliberate and resolute decision of the will; and from this cementing of minds, by God's decree, there arises a sacred and inviolable bond."[2]

Finally, the natural conjugal union is sacred because it mystically foreshadows the Hypostatic Union of the Divine and human natures in the mystery and miracle of the Incarnation of the Son of God and the Church, which is a figure of the Mystical Body of Christ. Little did Adam realize that God spoke in prophecy when He said, "Wherefore, a man shall leave father and mother, and shall cleave to his wife, and they shall be two in one flesh."[3]

"Christ, the eternal Son of God, coming into this world, wedded His Divinity to our humanity. He took to Himself our humanity, in order that we might participate in His Divinity. From this union we have the Incarnation; through the Incarnation the Redemption, through the Redemption the graces that come to us. He is the stem of the vine, we the branches invigorated by the sap of life which flows from the stem. This complete and supernatural union between Christ and His Spouse is called the Church."[4]

In his encyclical, *Casti Connubii,* Pope Pius XI quotes and enlarges upon the thoughts of his predecessor Pope Leo XIII when he wrote:

"That even natural wedlock has within it something that is sacred and religious can be established on grounds of natural reason alone, as shown in ancient historical documents, in the unvarying conscience of peoples, and in their institutions and customs. And this religious character of marriage is 'not adventitious but inherent in it, not humanly invented but naturally intrinsic to it,' because 'it has God as its author and because from the beginning it has been a *foreshadowing* of the Incarnation of the Word of God'."[5]

Pope Pius XI continued on his own:

"The sacred character of marriage, intimately connected with the sphere of religion and holy things, arises from its Divine origin already described; it arises also from its purpose, which is to beget and form children for God and to unite husband and wife with God by charity and mutual help; it arises, finally, from the natural function of marriage, instituted by the wise Providence of God the Creator to be a vehicle for the transmission of life, wherein parents act as ministers of the Divine Omnipotence."[6]

Pope Paul VI also speaks of the sacralized nature of the natural marriage contract in *Humanae Vitae*:

> "Married love particularly reveals its true nature and nobility when we realize that it derives from God and finds its supreme origin in Him who 'is Love,'[7] the Father 'from Whom every family in Heaven and Earth is named.'[8]...It is in reality the wise and provident institution of God the Creator, Whose purpose was to establish in man His loving design. As a consequence, husband and wife, through that mutual gift of themselves, which is specific and exclusive to them alone, developed that union of two persons in which they perfect one another, in order to cooperate with God in the generation and education of new lives."[9]

More splendid in holiness than the God-established natural contract is that very contract elevated by Christ to the dignity of Sacrament. Once Incarnate, the Second Person of the Most Blessed Trinity selected a marriage feast as the occasion for the sacramentalization of marriage. There was a marriage in Cana of Galilee and Mary was there. Jesus and His disciples were also invited to the marriage. When the wine failed, the Mother of Jesus said to Him, "They have no wine," and then she told the waiters, "Whatsoever he saith unto you, do it." Jesus had them fill the water pots and then asked them to take the water to the chief steward of the feast. When the chief steward had tasted it, he called the bridegroom and said to him: "Every man at the beginning doth set forth good wine; and when men have well drunk, then that which is worse: but thou hast kept the good wine until now." This miracle at Cana in Galilee was the first of Jesus' miracles. [10] Yet wonderful as is the physical miracle of the change of water into wine at Cana, more wonderful indeed is the less obvious miracle at Cana in the mystical order of reality. Water is a work of God alone, a good thing, a necessary thing, for the maintenance of natural life; wine is the work of God and man in cooperative effort, a good thing, a luxury which contributes to the joy of human life.

The Good Wine of Cana In Matrimony

Marriage, as a natural contract, is comparable to water, a creation of God at the beginning of time — given as a good thing, a necessary thing for the salvation of man and woman. Matrimony, the natural contract elevated to the dignity of Sacrament, can be likened to wine for it is that many-splendored thing which is the work of the Divinity and humanity of Christ at the beginning of His public life assuring the baptized direct flow of graces for the sanctity of the spouses. In the Old Testament, the natural contract of marriage, like the wine first served at the wedding feast of Cana, was good but not good enough to make saints of men and women on pilgrimage to Heaven. Christ in the New Testament, who said, "I am not come to destroy, but to fulfill," [11] took the good wine of the natural contract and gives only those men and women who believe in Him and are baptized in His name the better wine of the Sacrament which not only challenges the spouses to become greater saints of God but actually infuses those graces by which they can attain the highest reaches of spiritual perfection.

Leo XIII declared:

"Marriage is a Sacrament, because it is a holy sign which gives grace, showing forth an image of the mystical nuptials of Christ with the Church. But the form and image of these nuptials are shown precisely by the very bond of that close union which man and woman are bound together in one; which bond is nothing else but the marriage itself. Hence, it is clear that among Christians every true marriage is, in itself and by itself, a Sacrament; and that nothing can be further from the truth than to say that the Sacrament is a certain added ornament, or outward endowment, which can be separated and torn away from the contract at the caprice of man."[12]

Pius XI spoke along the same vein when he declared:

"The dignity of chaste wedlock will be best appreciated…if we consider that when Christ Our Lord, the Son of the Eternal Father, assumed the nature of fallen man, He was not content with giving a special place to marriage (the source and foundation of the family and therefore of human society) in the loving plan by which He completely restored our race; He did more: having re-established it in the perfection in which it had been originally instituted by God He raised it to the rank of a true and great Sacrament of the New Law, and accordingly entrusted the entire regulation and care of it to His Bride the Church."[13]

In another section of the encyclical he added:

"...new dignity is added by the Sacrament, by reason of which Christian wedlock has become by far the noblest marriage of all, being raised to such lofty eminence that the Apostle sees in it 'a great mystery,' and a thing 'honorable in all.'[14] The fact that marriage is a religious thing, that it is a sublime symbol of grace and of the union of Christ with His Church, makes it the duty of those contemplating marriage to treat Christian wedlock with holy reverence and to strive earnestly to make their future union approximate as closely as possible to its prototype."[15]

St. Paul compares the union between husband and wife to the union between Christ and His Spouse, the Church. The Apostle says: "...Husbands, love your wives, even as Christ also loved the church, and gave himself for it; That he might sanctify and cleanse it....So ought men to love their wives as their own bodies. He that loveth his wife loveth himself....This is a great mystery: but I speak concerning Christ and the church"[16] When St. Paul speaks of marriage as a "great mystery," he does not use the word in a strictly technical sense. What he means is that matrimony is a great sign of something holy, a mystical symbol of the union between Christ and His Church.

God saw that it was not good for man to be alone so He cast a deep sleep upon Adam in order to create Eve out of his very flesh. As Adam was made weak that Eve might be given to him to be his strength, so the Son of God, the second Adam, became weak, emptying Himself of Himself so that He might take upon Himself the form of a servant and clothed in flesh might accomplish total victory over sin and death. As Eve was taken from the side of Adam during his sleep and became the mother of all living, so the Church taken from the side of Christ as He slept upon the cross became for Him His one and only chosen spouse, the mother of all those to whom He had come to give life. This union between Christ and His Church is effected by sanctifying grace; it continues by the constant flow of all those graces necessary for the attainment of the purpose of the Church, namely, the salvation of all souls. If, therefore, the bond of matrimony is like the bond between Christ and His Church, it is the Christ-given means by which graces which sanctify the married state are conferred to those baptized in His name.

A Sacrament is a sacred sensible sign instituted by Christ to signify and to confer grace. Since matrimony is a Sacrament, it is a sensible sign. The matter and form of the Sacrament make up the sensible sign. In the natural contract of marriage, man and woman as created by God were the matter and their consent was the form; in the Sacrament it is the regenerated man and woman, the validly baptized man and woman, the Christed man and Christed woman who comprise the sacred matter and their consent spoken in the presence of the minister of the Church which is the form. Baptism, that Christ-given Sacrament, which initiates human beings into the very companionship, the very family of the Trinity, gives ennoblement to the human beings who give their total consent "for better or worse, for richer or poorer, and in sickness and health," until death do they part.

The splendor of the Sacrament flows from and into Christ Who instituted it, according to the Fathers of the Church, on the occasion of the wedding feast of Cana of Galilee, but more assuredly so instituted, according to theologians on the occasion of the Sermon on the Mount when He restored the natural contract of marriage to its original dignity given it by His Father.[17] It is because Christ is God that this sacramentalized institution now becomes the channel of those husband-wife, father-mother graces so essential for the happiness of spouses in time and blessedness preparing them for Eternity. All this proclaims that matrimony is no longer the water of the Old Law but it is the wine of the

New Law. It is that good wine given by the Father in Paradise that now is the better wine tasted and drunk in full draughts by Christed souls so long as they live together and in preparation for the glory of the Kingdom to come.

From the fact that Christ raised the natural marriage contract to the dignity of a Sacrament, it follows that the parties themselves are the ministers of the Sacrament. The priest is not the minister of the Sacrament but only the official witness of it, in keeping with the sublime words of the first Pope of the Church, Peter, who spoke of all those baptized as a "chosen generation, a kingly priesthood, a holy nation, a purchased people"[18] that those men and women who have been Christianed are really participating in the unordained or common priesthood of Christ. It is the baptized man and the baptized woman who hand themselves over to each other making a mutual contract to live together until death. It is the baptized man and baptized woman therefore, who confer on each other the Sacrament enabling them to fulfill the higher duties which are involved in the Christian marriage state. It is the man who, as God's minister, confers on the woman those soul beauties which make her a figure of the Church, the Bride of Christ. And likewise, it is the woman, who as God's minister, confers on the man those soul beauties which make him a figure of Christ, the Bridegroom of the Church. Husband and wife are thus the complement of each other in their supernatural, as well as in their natural, relationships. Once again the water of the old dispensation now becomes the wine of the new dispensation — the better wine of the Church, that Cana which is the shadow of the bright Cana prepared for those who are faithful to each other in life and in death.

Inviolable Union

St. Augustine, in delineating the blessings of Christian marriage named three: offspring (*prolis*), conjugal fidelity (*fides*), and the Sacrament (*Sacramentum*). Pope Pius XI says: "…the complement and crown of all is a blessing of Christian marriage which, following St. Augustine, we have called Sacrament. It denotes both the indissolubility of the matrimonial bond, and the consecration of this contract by Christ, Who elevated it to the rank of a sign which is a cause of grace."[19] Since something has already been said about the elevation of the natural contract of marriage to the dignity of a Sacrament, it remains for something to be said about that last blessing described by the great Augustine. The indissolubility of matrimony was emphatically declared by Christ Himself in the words: "What therefore God hath joined together, let no man put asunder"[20] and "Every one that putteth away his wife and marrieth another committeth adultery: and he that marrieth her that is put away from her husband committeth adultery."[21]

What Our Lord had said was nothing novel or original. This inviolable stability, this attribute was already spoken of by the Creator concerning the nuptial union of Adam and Eve, our first parents, the prototype of all future marriages and consequently applicable to every true marriage. The perfection and strictness of the original law of permanence were modified in the Old Testament only because of the hardness of the hearts of God's people and announced as such by Moses for only specific cases. Christ, in virtue of His power as Supreme Legislator, revoked this confession and restored the law to its original perfection by the words which must never be forgotten, "What God had joined together let no man put asunder."

St. Paul in addressing a group of Greeks at Corinth among whom were many of his converts, spoke out boldly against adultery and divorce. Some had husbands or wives who were still far from Christian, and as such still with pagan laxity of morals in married life. The Apostle of the Gentiles found the Romans no better than the Greeks to whom he preached. Without mincing words he wrote to them: "For the woman that hath an husband, whilst her husband liveth is bound to the law. But if her husband be dead, she is loosed from the law of her husband. Therefore, whilst her husband liveth, she shall be called an adulteress, if she be with another man."[22] St. Augustine follows through when he speaks of this great blessing called Sacrament: "Sacrament signifies that the bond of wedlock shall never be broken, and that neither party, if separated, shall form a union with another, even for the sake of offspring."[23]

Pius VI wrote:

> "Wherefore it is evident that even in the state of nature, and at all events long before it was raised to the dignity of a Sacrament properly so-called, marriage was Divinely constituted in such a way as to involve a perpetual and indissoluble bond, which consequently cannot be dissolved by a civil law. Therefore, although a marriage may exist without the Sacrament, as in the case of marriage between infidels, even so, being a true marriage it must and does retain the character of a perpetual bond, which from the very beginning has been by Divine Law inseparable from marriage and over which no civil power has any authority. Therefore if a marriage is said to be contracted, either it is so contracted as to be a true marriage, in which case it carries with it that perpetual bond which by Divine Law is inherent in every true marriage; or else it is deemed to be contracted without this perpetual bond, in which case it is not a true marriage at all, which consequently may not be entered upon or maintained."[24]

For 1500 years after Christ had spoken the words in defense of the permanence of matrimony, restoring the original contract of marriage to the high dignity given it by God in Paradise, all Christians looked upon that sacred bond as one which can only be broken by death. The first attack on the sanctity of the permanence of matrimony was an exterior one; it came from those who were in high places. There came on the historical scene the so-called Reformers in the sixteenth century who began to wrest Christ's words to their own destruction, to suit their own passions. King Henry VIII of England repudiated the Faith, set up his own religion, and precipitated the bloody persecutions which followed, because Pope Clement VII would not grant him a divorce from his lawful wife. So England fell away from the Church.

Napoleon forsook his devoted wife Josephine to marry Marie

Louise of Austria. He did not even consult Pope Pius VII because he knew his appeal for divorce would be fruitless. Pope Pius VII adamantly stated to Napoleon: "We cannot utter a judgment in opposition to the rules of the Church, and we could not, without laying aside those rules, decree the invalidity of a union which, according to the Word of God, no human power can sunder." Napoleon's apostasy was followed by a persecution of the Church during which even the Pope was thrown into prison. And much of France was lost to the Church.

The New Paganism

The Popes, as custodians of the sacredness of marriage, must rather see whole nations apostatize than prove disloyal to the sacred trust given them by Christ. Pope Pius XI lamented over the sad situation in our modern times:

> "The chief obstacle to the renovation and rehabilitation of marriage willed by Christ the Redeemer lies...in the constantly increasing facility of divorce. The advocates of the new paganism, undeterred by the lessons of a sad experience, persist in an unrelenting spirit of hostility to the sacred indissolubility of wedlock and to the legislation which protects it. They are untiring in their efforts to obtain the legal authorization of divorce, and to substitute for the out-of-date legislation of the past a law which will be more humane."[25]

In our times, now that the floodgates for divorce have been thrown open by government leaders, the torrential flood of divorce threatens to engulf all society. The desacralization of marriage is spreading not only among pagans [and] those who call themselves Christians, but among those who claim to be Catholic. The attack on the sacred permanence of marriage also comes from within its very bosom, that is to say from the husband and wife who had either contracted marriage or received the Sacrament of Matrimony.

Young men and young women who fall in love, are all too often blind, deaf, and mute before their marriage; after a few years, sometimes even after a few months, they regain their sight, hearing, and speech. Since no two human beings have ever been compatible they begin to discover rationalizations to prove their incompatibility to each other the easier and sooner to ask the State to sever their marriage bond. The tragedy is made even more tragic because their consciences are undisturbed by the moral ruin they bring into their respective lives and to the common good of society.

How often a young man and young woman pronounce their marriage vows unrealistically. Sometimes with stars in their eyes and music in their ears they repeat, "I, take you for better, for richer, for health," without remembering the words "until death do us part"; sometimes with lightning in their eyes and thunder in their ears they repeat, "I take you for worse, for poorer, and for sickness," without recalling the words "until death do us part." In their immaturity they either want only roses, sunshine, and running laughter or they anticipate only thorns, rain, and running tears.

The first quarrel which hurts their selfishness makes the man and woman, without any reference to the Incarnation of Jesus Christ, forget that God is the Author of marriage, and that together they were to move toward God through good times and bad times in their married life. The baptized man and woman cannot disjoint the unity of their marriage and make it a temporary arrangement any more than Christ can now disjoint His Divinity from His humanity fused together in Hypostatic Union as it was at the time of His Incarnation. In moments of self-centeredness the baptized man and woman do not wish to be reminded that it was the Son of God Who raised marriage to the dignity of a Sacrament, refuse to cooperate with the graces it gave them, do not avert to the sacerdotal function they performed when they exchanged their vows, only to jeopardize their eternal destiny in Heaven. The Christian man and woman cannot tear asunder their union and cast aside the permanence of their marriage bond any more than Christ, the Bridegroom, can abandon the Church, His one and only mystic bride to whom He is wedded for all eternity for He pledged to be with her even unto the consummation of the world.

Christ came into this world to sacralize all creation. In a sublime sense, like King Midas who turned everything he touched into gold, Christ Jesus touched the contract of marriage and changed it into a Sacrament. The Church, which is the prolongation and extension of Christ in history and geography, has the same function of making sacrosanct everything which falls under her sway. That is why she is constantly bestowing Sacraments and why she is always blessing all things as sacramentals. To her matrimony is forever something resplendent with holiness and she will always come to the defense of its unity and indissolubility. As in the past, so now and in the future she will remind nations and peoples that their governments must return to the acceptance of the primeval concept of the sanctity of marriage and allow the Church full authority over the Sacrament. Civil authorities could do nothing more blessed than to completely outlaw divorce and eliminate its possibilities in protective legislation.

Pope Pius XI counseled the married wisely when he spoke:

"…Husband and wife must make and keep this sacred and solemn resolution: that in all things concerning marriage they will without any hesitation keep the commandments of God; help each other always in mutual love; preserve the honor of chastity; never violate the indissolubility of the marriage bond; and use their matrimonial rights always in a Christian spirit.... For forming, maintaining, and fulfilling this resolution, Christian husbands and wives will find great assistance in frequent meditation upon their state and in an effective remembrance of the Sacrament they have received. Let them be constantly mindful that they have been consecrated and strengthened for the duties and dignity of their state by a Sacrament whose efficacy, though it does not confer a character, remains nonetheless in perpetuity. In this connection they will do well to ponder these consoling words of the saintly Cardinal Bellarmine: 'The Sacrament of matrimony may be considered in two ways: in the moment of its accomplishment, and in its permanency afterwards. This Sacrament, in fact, is similar to the Eucharist, which, likewise, is a Sacrament not only in a moment of its accomplishment, but also as long as it remains. For as long as husband and wife live, their fellowship is always the Sacrament of Christ and the Church'."[26]

Those in marriage must revere the Sacrament in all the vicissitudes of their wedded life, remembering they have taken each other for better or for worse, for richer or for poorer, in sickness and in health, until death do they part. God will never be wanting to their needs. He will give them in the Sacrament all husband-wife, father-mother graces "in a measure pressed down and overflowing." The water of routine, the day in and day out gray sameness, the monotony will be turned into the better wine of holiness in time and eternity.

ENDNOTES

1.   *Gen.* 1:26
2.   Pope Pius XI, *Christian Marriage,* Catholic Truth Society, London, 1964, n.7.
3.   *Gen.* 2:24
4.   Rev. Clement Crock, *Discourses on Grace and the Sacraments*, Joseph F. Wagner, Inc., New York City, 1940, p. 257.
5.   Leo XIII, *Arcanum*, 1880.
6.   Pius XI, *op. cit.,* n.82.
7.   *I John* 4:8.
8.   *Ephesians* 3:15.
9.   Pope Paul VI, *The Regulation of Birth*, Catholic Truth Society, London, 1968, n.8
10. *John* 2:1-11
11. *Matthew* 5:17.
12. Leo XIII, *op.cit.*
13. *Christian Marriage*, n.1.
14. *Ephesians* 5:32; *Hebrews* 13:4.
15. *Christian Marriage*, n. 82-83.
16. *Ephesians* 5:25-26, 28, 32.
17. *Matthew* 5:27ff; cf. *Matthew* 19:3ff.
18. *I Peter* 2:9.
19. *Christian Marriage*, n.31.
20. *Matthew* 19:6.
21. *Luke* 16:18.
22. *Romans* 7:2-3.
23. Augustine, *De Gen.ad litt.,* lib. IX, cap.7, N.12.
24. Pius VI, *Recript . ad Episc. Agriens*, July 11, 1789.
25. *Christian Marriage*, n.87.
26. *Ibid.,* n.115-116.

Rt. Rev. Msgr. Alphonse Popek delivered this address at the Ninth National Wanderer Forum. Msgr. Popek served as a priest of the Archdiocese of Milwaukee from 1939 until his death in 1976. In 1947, he earned his doctorate in Canon Law from Catholic University and he taught Canon Law for 16 years at St. Francis Seminary. He served as moderator of the Apostolate of Suffering and, in 1962, became the national spiritual director of the Pious Union of the Sick. He organized priestly fraternities, worked in diocesan offices as defender of the bond, promotor of justice, and prosynodal judge. He was known for championing priestly celibacy and the rights of the unborn.

THE VIRTUE OF MARRIED CHASTITY

Dr. William A. Marra
Butler, New Jersey

I don't have to elaborate on the fact that the entire decadence of the twentieth century in Western countries revolves around marriage. The pornography, the extra-marital sex, the flippant way in which marriage itself is treated — all point to this disease afflicting the right understanding of sex and marriage.

Let's begin, however, not with any profound observation but with a simple, single, obvious fact that we really don't need courses in sex education to teach people, and yet this fact is at basis of the entire topic of Christian Marriage and the basis of all human life. The fact is simply this, we humans – we human persons – come in two different versions, male and female. And that sounds so basic and so obvious, of course, that I ask you to reflect what sort of a science-fiction horror story we could write if it weren't so. Just imagine the world all men or all women, and you could see the real horror and the great changes that would have to be made on the face of the earth. So it is to this basic, if you will, biological fact, that I first address myself because I want you to understand one kind of activity which individual men and individual women engage in, the activity, namely, of uniting in marriage. It is an ancient tradition found in all cultures, always with some relationship to religion. It is, in any case, the topic of even behavioral science which looks upon it as one more instinct rooted in the human race

First of all, we will focus on this institution called marriage to ask these questions: What really belongs to the essence of marriage; and of course, what is this essence of Christian marriage, since marriage itself, apart from the Sacrament, is already a profound and important reality in the human race.

Second, what difference does marriage make to sexual inter-course? The French have a very excellent way of formulating the Ninth Commandment. We say, "Thou shall not covet thy neighbor's wife." But the French say, "Thou shalt not seek the work of the flesh outside marriage." That's an extremely happy formulation of what the commandment says, "Thou shall not seek the work of the flesh outside marriage." And my question is: What magic does marriage have which makes the work of the flesh *within* marriage morally acceptable, *outside* of marriage a terrible impurity?

My third topic will very briefly note the demands of fidelity within marriage which marriage itself makes upon the partners – never mind now the work of the flesh outside marriage but now that we *are* married, what are the demands of fidelity. And finally, I will allude to something which is not too often noted and yet which is a very important part of our understanding of marriage, namely, the role that death plays in marriage and in love.

I speak from a God-centered view, that being a Christian and being certified even by the Wanderer Forum, I act from the knowledge and conviction that a personal God exists. And you might say, What other alternative might one act on? Well, as we all know the rage today, even among so-called Christians, is – even if God is admitted to exist – to *postpone* God's providence in the world, to act as if God might in some way be necessary to *start* the world going (insisting on evolution, arbitrary chance, blind forces, impulses, which after a hundred tries or a million tries finally managed to get the world made).

But we who believe in God, believe as follows, that a personal Creator with reason, with infinite wisdom and understanding broods over the creation. That there's nothing accidental even in the color of a rose, even in the fact that sunsets are beautiful, but even these things speak deep messages from God. Still less is there anything accidental in that basic fact that we come in two versions, man and woman. It is not a twist of evolution, not one of these happy accidents which allows the human race to enjoy itself a bit that we come in two sexual versions — male and female — but rather because the providence and wisdom and will of God willed it so. And our attitude therefore should be one of reverently probing part of the meaning of this mystery that we human persons, ultimately made by God, are so structured as to be complementary in the different sexual roles.

Permanence

The essence of marriage is my first point and I will not labor this point; we all know it, but I should like to enumerate what marriage is not, so that we can appreciate the ideal. Marriage is not the love between a man and a woman, however deep this love might be. Hopefully this love precedes marriage, is the motive for marriage, informs the marriage, flourishes in the marriage. Let us pray that a concrete marriage be so vivified by this love between the man and the woman, but we all admit that even the great love, even a requited love, is not yet marriage.

Secondly, marriage is not any sexual intimacy which is, of course, the fashion of the young thinkers in the universities. They say that we have this new lifestyle of sharing sleeping arrangements between the sexes, and they even share the cooking and the laundry and so on and they're very honest about it. But this is not marriage, it is concubinage, fornication: it is not marriage. We must say that what marriage is and what we all know marriage to be, the essence of marriage, is not the voice of the heart, which is love; it is not the intimacy of the body which is sexual union; but the heart of marriage is in this case, the act of will, the vow, the consensus, the pledge that each makes to each to constitute a permanent union. And we have always been taught this and we always know this and we've even been taught that strictly speaking a marriage is real, and valid even without a preacher, in that old far-fetched example of two people shipwrecked on a desert island and the priest won't be there for another six years. Well then, you can marry yourself. That's far-fetched, but the principle is valid that what constitutes marriage is no ceremony as such, no liturgy as such – not bell, book, candle, still less expensive wedding receptions and flowers and bridal gowns, however much these are important and help to emphasize the solemnity of marriage – but that the heart of marriage is this solid pledge of each to each, to enter into a permanent union.

Shakespeare gives us a hint on why this pledge is so important, and life itself and its experiences give us more than a hint. Shakespeare says somewhere that "men are April when they woo and December when they wed," and I think we can appreciate the force of that, that there are these exhilarating moments in life when we love a person or think we love a person, when there's this excitement and admiration of another when April blossoms in the heart and then marriage or the valid marriage is just this somewhat heroic promise made in the good times that even if December sets in, we will be pledged to one together. That, as Chesterton said so well, the man who makes any vow, and that includes the religious vows or the vow of marriage, makes an appointment with himself in some future time and place so that even in my youth and in my enthusiasm, when my heart says yea to the woman, I nevertheless with my will, freely, solemnly, earnestly, seriously pledge this bond of fidelity against the future when the heart might waiver, when conditions might change, and when I don't want to keep that appointment with myself.

So let us recognize this heroic element which really needs some sort of justification because it is so extraordinary that we pledge our lives together in this moment in a free decision. What we pledge is to enter into an institution, into a way of life, that has a structure of its own.

The Popes that are especially concerned with Christian marriage, Paul VI in *Humanae Vitae* and Pius XI in *Casti Connubii,* both stress the point – but especially Pius XI – that marriage has a nature of its own, it's already structured, it's already a God-given essence, and the freedom of man does not apply to tampering with the essence of marriage. Rather the freedom of man is limited to this: that we freely resolve to enter this structure, we freely accept the invitation to enter this garden of permanence. But to repeat, the essence of marriage is precisely this mutual consent of the two spouses.

Now when I make this point, it's important to note a modern confusion based somewhat on this point, which certain young people are in favor of now and which seems to be so intelligent and so honest because they seem to be saying the same thing as I. I've just said awhile ago that the essence of marriage is the commitment, is the vow, it is not necessarily the preacher or the bridal gown or the wedding reception. And you hear young people saying that too, and even people not so young, but what they're saying is quite different from my point.

Here's a typical case and this actually happened to me a year ago. This young college sophomore came up to me and very openly and honestly said, "Oh yes, Doc, Laura and I are living together. We're not going to hide this, we're very honest." And I am rather used to this now so I didn't exactly show myself shocked, but he felt impelled to defend himself. He said, "We don't need those formalities, those bits of paper, the license, the Wasserman tests, the ceremony, and so on. We are too mature for that."

Now I so far have nothing against this and I think it would be wrong to oppose this argument by saying: "Yes, yes, John but you broke your mother's heart, because she wanted a big reception and she wanted the daughter-in-law to have a big floral bouquet," and so on as if you take issue with this concubinage merely because it omitted the ceremony.

No, I said to this young man: "Of course John you didn't have the piece of paper and the priest and so on, but you did *vow* in private to live together permanently. You did, in the sight of God, pledge fidelity and life together, didn't you?" Now had he said "Yes," then I could not really accuse him of much, except disobedience to Church law, and of course, to civil law. But at least he could philosophically have been clean, at least he could say: "I'm tired of all these formalities, I'm tired of all this modern phoniness and expense and so on. But in this ultimate authenticity of my life I vow to live with this girl and she with me and we seal this promise in the name of God."

That could philosophically be considered a marriage, although I repeat, it is sinful in that it neglects the Sacrament and it is also probably illegal, if anything can be illegal today.

But what did this young man say to me? Just the opposite. And what he said so many other people say: "Oh no, we didn't make any pledge of any kind," he said. "My goodness, how can we tell how we're going to feel two years from now." And he even got nervous, "Six months from now."

And that's the heart of the issue. The real heart of the issue, dear friends, is not whether you reject or accept ceremony, flowers; it's whether you reject or accept the *vow*, the pledge of fidelity, the honest promise that there will be insurance, as it were, against the possible Decembers of your life. This is a victory really over the future in the solemn vow made in the present. Therefore this man and his friend were not married in a hippie sense. They were in concubinage as are so many.

The Work of the Flesh

I come now to this second point about this question of extra-marital and pre-marital sex, this whole question of thou shalt not seek the work of the flesh outside marriage – and as you know this has certainly become problematic in the Church. The latest insights in the behavioral sciences and the latest insights of the new theology and the latest sensitivity session of Fr. Sick and Sr. Crazy have suddenly made unintelligible any sort of clarity about sexual decency; that suddenly the question is raised: Just what is wrong with this wholesome expression of ourselves? And then marriage is seen to be a kind of empty formality. They ask: "What is there magical about a few words exchanged in front of a preacher or in front of the justice of the peace which somehow legitimates this bodily union?" And that's a valid question. That is, we ought to pause, and ask ourselves: What exactly does the vow do to the question of purity in sexual relations? I've already hinted at the answer that this vow implies there is no trifling with the other. This vow implies a free acceptance of an institution to which alone it belongs that certain activities are not only permitted but encouraged.

There are three things to be united really: namely love – the love between the man and the woman; sexual intercourse – the bodily union between the two; and marriage – the promise made between the two. And as we know only too well certain of these can exist without the other. We have sex without marriage, love without sex, in every possible combination, and every once in a while, we have marriage and love and sex, which is good news for some people that it can happen and it does happen.

This is one of the most difficult topics to speak on for the simple reason that there is no possible scientific way to understand marriage as you might understand magnetism or blood circulation. Normally there is an object in nature which functions in a certain way and the scientist simply scrutinizes how the thing functions and he simply discovers regularities and laws of magnetism or blood circulation. And some people try to do the same with marriage. You have the social scientists with their microscopic vision and they scrutinize this type of living together and that lifestyle and this lifestyle and then they come up with very deep laws and very deep regularities about how the typical middle-class marriage works out, and what the typical concubinage consists in, and the typical Black marriage and White marriage and Chicano marriage and they act as if they're being scientists in noticing what's happening.

But I claim when it comes to an institution which is above all a spiritual thing, an essence – something willed by God but not necessarily realized by man – it is simply trivial to examine what is happening. Rather should we ask what *ought* to happen. Given that there are men and women, given that there is such a thing as love between the sexes, given that there is such a thing as the whole question of human sexuality, then what is the ideal, what ought to be, are the questions we are to ask ourselves. In other words: What is the God-given meaning of marriage?

Unity is the Essence

And my dear teacher, Dietrich von Hildebrand, I maintain, almost alone of writers in the West, certainly within the last hundred years, has undertaken many brilliant writings precisely on this meaning of marriage, not the *de facto* marriage with its many unhappinesses and its many questions, but what marriage ought to be, the God-given essence of it. And against that essence he measures the concrete marriage to see how far it departs from the ideal, and against that essence he begins to understand the horror of impurity. And may I urge everyone here again if you do not know von Hildebrand's works on marriage and purity, may I urge that you procure them and read them. He has more to say than any man I have ever read, including St. Augustine on this question of purity.

Let me therefore look for a moment at what ought to be, what is this God-willed essence or ideal of marriage and, by the way, I speak not yet of Christian marriage. But I say it's valid even for those who do not know Christ, and Christian marriage simply transfigures the natural marriage, elevates it, but does not destroy it, it simply brings it to its fulfillment.

First of all, very briefly, I will numerate the ingredients to this ideal. The first ingredient is the love, the love between the sexes, this earnest love which a man feels for a woman or a woman for a man. This love has not always been stressed in teaching of marriage. One has sometimes referred to it merely as a friendship or harmony or getting along, but I say that experience teaches us and also literature and also history, that there exists such a thing as this ardent attraction between the sexes, and happy the person who has at least known this even if it has not worked out. He begins to understand the depths of experience, he begins to measure the work of all other kinds against this noble aspiration of the heart.

Now when we have this love between the sexes let us admit, let us understand the moment a man yearns for unity with the woman he loves. He yearns for unity of heart, that she loves him back, that she requite the love. He yearns for a unity of life – it is an insufferable thought that he live apart from the loved one – and he yearns for a unity of body. That, as von Hildebrand shows, the love between the sexes is not itself sexual but of the spirit, of the heart, and yet it finds its completion in the body, in the sexual embrace, even in the kiss. The kiss and the sexual embrace are the signs and the completion, the bodily completion of the love that ought to exist in the first place.

I think also that when a man loves a woman he looks upon marriage, not as some trap, not as some legal document which he must reluctantly sign in order to have his way. Quite the contrary, he thinks marriage is the most privileged state. What a happiness for him that the one he loves will freely consent to bind her destiny with his own. Therefore let us in our depths appreciate there are very few shotgun marriages, as it were. We're not really forced or prodded into marriage, we yearn for it, we are grateful for this noble institution and, if it did not exist, we'd invent it because it answers so fully the voice of love pleading for permanence, pleading for dedication, life together.

I think also of the intimacy of the sexual sphere and this is a part of sex which is completely unknown among the sex educators today. They see no difference between the tonsils and the sexual parts of a man's body, that they have this pseudo-scientific way of looking at the body as of one piece. Whereas anyone who understands the slightest thing about his own nakedness or his own body, knows that the sexual parts of a body represent the inner sanctum of a man. They represent the intimate part of the human life and it is because of this intimacy that it may not be publicly displayed, that it ought not be publicly lavished on anyone else, that my sexual part is my secret to be revealed to the loved one, to be given to the loved one, not to be flaunted before every taxi driver or clerk in the store. I might say not only ought we not to seek the work of the flesh outside marriage, we ought not display the wares of sex outside marriage, that it belongs to the spouse to see our nakedness not to the people on the beach or on the bus.

And I think finally of the fruitfulness of sex, that upon the occasion of a bodily union between a man and a woman, a new person, an immortal soul, an identity which God alone fashions comes into being. And therefore I stand in awe of sex because of its intimate quality and because of its fruitfulness.

It Is the Vow That Makes the Difference

Now, putting these things together, I ask: What does the vow mean? What does the marriage vow have to do with sex and love and intimacy? It simply means this: that hopefully, the vow is made because of love – that would be devoutly wished, that no person promises life together except he loves the other. But even if there is no love on one side or another or even if there is an imperfect love which we are only too willing to grant to our fallen nature, nevertheless the vow – even the natural vow but above all the Christian vow of the sacramental marriage – it means simply that we have abandoned each our single lives, we freely will to enter the circle of intimacy which is marriage, we freely will to reveal our nakedness and to yield our bodies to the other.

It is the vow which makes this decisive difference, that we will leave father and mother, we will cleave to another in a life of intimacy and permanency; the vow indicates our decision, our earnestness that we trifle not with another, that this is our God-willed partner – hopefully they say because of love, but even if love be lacking or diminished, it is this earnestness which makes all the difference between the pure use of sex and the impure use of sex: Sex outside of the vow is a trifling, a

squandering, a letting go of one's self. The inner sanctum ought not to be revealed to the casual partner, to the date, to the dormitory partner. It ought to be reserved for that life partner into whose intimate union we freely enter.

When I say this, a lot of people like it. Von Hildebrand is rather popular among young people whenever he lectures among college campuses because there is something invigorating about the notion of marriage for love and sex in wedded love – who could dispute this? And no person would really quarrel with that. And every once in a while, as I noted, it even happens that there are marriages full of it, and that there is sex taking place within marriage in a pure and chaste way and there is a child as a fruitful token of the union of the two.

But the big problem about the vow is simply this, that the very vow which invited us into the garden of marriage, the very vow which enabled us in God's eyes purely to reveal our nakedness to the other, it soon enough can become burdensome to us. In other words, it was April when we wooed and December when we wed. And Shakespeare says men are April when they woo and December when they're wed and, in the interest of equality, I might add women have their seasons too. This is the real problem, that the vow made in the enthusiasm of what was perhaps not a genuine love or a deep love, it soon becomes burdensome to us, above all, if after the solemn vow and valid marriage with another, we meet someone we really love. And then comes all this agitation for a new concept of marriage and so on, which we are witnessing in the Church today.

Fidelity and Death

Therefore, my next question is this: What does it mean that marriage involves fidelity between the two partners? And I note that it means at least this: that I have once said and meant that I will live a life together with this person, for this fidelity that I owe the other at least means this, that I will not commit adultery with a third party. This is the most obvious thing of marital fidelity, that I shall not seek the work of the flesh outside my marriage, that it is between my wife and me, not an adulterous union with another. But Christ warns us not only the deed but even the intention, the lusting after of someone not our spouse which constitutes adultery. So fidelity means secondly, therefore, to banish all thoughts of illicit union with that other person, with that third person. Fidelity means in the third place a positive attempt with my will to be loyal to my spouse, to understand the mystery of my vocation, the mystery of our intimacy, the possible children that have come from the bond, and it means I think and I contemplate upon those qualities in the spouse which at one time made me think I loved her and perhaps I still love her. So these are at least the implications of fidelity within marriage. It also finally means fidelity, loyalty to the bond, that to be a faithful spouse means to acknowledge that we have not the right and we have not the power to dissolve what we freely constituted. This is essential to understanding even natural marriage, but above all Christian marriage, because in Christian marriage we pledge fidelity to each other and hand the bond to Christ. He is the keeper of that bond. So to be a faithful spouse means I am faithful to the bond. To put it in Supreme Court language therefore, that the doctrine of marriage or fidelity in marriage means one man, one wife until death parts them. One man, one wife until death.

This is a hard saying and we ought to admit this that even in the Gospel when the Apostles spoke to Christ about adultery and divorce, Christ firmly insisted that once you're married you're forever married and if you ever put away your wife and marry another you are guilty of adultery. The Apostles said, well if this be so then it is expedient for us not to marry – because they understood the audacity really of a marriage vow which binds us forever until death parts. And I think we ought to admit that marriage has this possibility of happiness.

Bear Your EarthlyTrials

This leads me to my final point about the meaning of death with respect to marriage. We promise to love and to stay with the other until death parts us and this doctrine of death has two sides to it. Marriages are for better and for worse and when a marriage is for the worse as unfortunately many are, the doctrine of death should console us – this is a *profound* point, I am not advocating spousicide or something like that. We have Christ's words Himself that in the Resurrection they shall neither marry nor be given in marriage – they shall be as the angels of Heaven. Therefore to those unhappily married, the Church first of all tries to anticipate the unhappiness and bring you to your depths before you pledge; but if the Church has failed, you are consoled and are to be consoled by the thought that this vow you freely made is now your trial: bear with it manfully; and against the dimensions of eternity, it is not all that bad. If we want to use spatial analogies, eternity could be likened to a line one mile long and your earthly life a half inch. And with St. Paul, we could say I reckoned that the sufferings of this life are not worthy to be compared with the glory of the life to come.

But then this very consolation I give to those who are unhappily married, depresses those who are happily married because then they say and it happens, friends, there are people who have experienced the real joys of married love and married life and married fruitfulness and they must be saddened by the shadows of death and their great question is:

Will death, too, abolish this bond of fidelity which we have loved so much, which has been so blessed for us? And we must answer the bond will be abolished. Christ will not be gainsaid, death will cancel out the bond of marriage, but that other bond which you should have nurtured and probably did nurture in your marriage, that will endure forever.

Let me end on this thought in *Casti Connubii*, Pius XI, almost as an afterthought, after giving a very strict philosophy of the meaning of marriage, says in a remarkable passage that "the mutual interior formation of husband and wife is in a certain way the primary cause and reason of marriage." It's a very striking admission said in an offhanded way, as if children apart now, happiness apart now, the fact that within this marriage we confirm each other, we open up the channels of grace for each other, we help each other love God more – this is in a certain way, he said, the primary cause of marriage and I will note this although eternity insists that the bond of marriage will be erased, it will no longer be necessary, that love transfigured by charity, that love of God and love of the other in God – this will endure forever.

And if I might dare paraphrase Christ's words, it seems to me as if Christ will, if we are faithful, if we married persons are faithful to God, in that moment of ecstasy when we meet our Judge, He will say, "I know you *both*. I know you both," and He will say to us, "You two have been faithful in little things, enter now into the joys of the Lord *together.*"

Dr. William Marra delivered this opening address of the Ninth National Wanderer Forum in 1973. Dr. Marra completed his graduate studies under Dietrich von Hildebrand and taught philosophy at Fordham University in New York for several years. In addition he wrote for numerous publications and lectured on ethical questions including the problems of war, conflict of conscience and authority, and sex education in schools. He founded the Roman Forum at Fordham to discuss philosophical, theological, and ecclesiastical questions. Many of his talks are on audiocassettes. Dr. Marra died in 1998.

Photo by Charles Shipp

CHILDREN:
THE OUTSTANDING GIFT OF MARRIAGE

Dr. Reginald Gallop
Winnipeg, Manitoba, Canada

Dr. William Marra has given an excellent preamble to the nature of Christian Marriage, which is, of course, the crowning glory of all concepts of marriage in history – naturally enough, because God Himself, explicitly through His Divine Son, Our Lord Jesus Christ, so sanctified what was pre-Christian marriage to a point where we have these marvelous analogies for marriage which all the Popes and St. Augustine and the great Doctors von Hildebrand and Marra have given us. Christians must never forget these tremendous analogies, if they ever tend to have any debased view of what Christian Marriage is: Our Lord compared Christian Marriage in depth, scope, and sanctity, as far as human understanding can go, to the marriage between Him and His bride, the Church. This is something that is difficult to understand, but it is something we must look up to, as an extremely deep and extremely inspiring source of meditation should we ever run into any of those difficult situations which Dr. Marra explained to us. Just prior to my own wedding, I remember a wise old man associated with me in Tasmania said, "Well son, if your marriage is successful, there's nothing like it." And he said, "Boy, if it's not successful, there's still nothing like it."

In relation to Dr. Marra's remarks about those who have the bad luck to throw the wrong dice, and when our hearts override our wisdom and our minds (which is a problem of man since Eve who caused her rational husband to be emotional rather than rational, and he fell for it. And of course, we have had lots of problems since), Our Lord came along later and said, to commiserate with those whom Dr. Marra describes and whom we know, "Take up your cross and carry it!" And don't we know what that means, in the human marriage sense, as well as others.

The Total Picture

As a background, I must introduce the total picture: God the Majestic, Perfect, Infinite Creator made our universe and filled it with a wonderful, harmonious mosaic of natural order and beauty. And then He delegated the proper management of a small part of it to man. Remember that the Earth is an insignificantly small part of creation. That's where we are, that's where we will remain, except as visitors to nearby space. A few weeks away, a few months away, maybe a few years away is all we'll ever go into in space, for various reasons, particularly of human physiology. It's very interesting to realize that our little planet is so insignificant in the cosmos. In astronomy, it really can be discounted, as there are so many, and much larger planets, and far beyond — millions of light years away. It takes great scientific skill to detect the locations of some of these distant bodies which God made, which God alone sees, and which God alone will ever see, except by man in a pale reflection through a telescope or through a space probe. We have been put on this little tiny, geographical part of creation with a special role and a special destiny as described so well in Genesis. It's very sobering to meditate for a moment on that.

God delegated the proper management of this small part of His creation deliberately, lovingly, and hopefully to His priceless, beloved, human sons and daughters, whom He made uniquely in His image, each with a mighty spark of the Divine Nature in them. Each one of us has been specially appointed into existence by God. None of us apply for existence. None of us *can* apply for existence. We are only appointed into existence. And correspondingly, we are appointed out of existence, as I'll explain in a little more detail later.

We have been appointed into existence uniquely by God, in cooperation with our human parents. Each of us is unique, and our parents are unique. When the twenty-three chromosomes from each parent unite to form a new person, with the infusion of the soul of that unique person, from the reservoir of souls in the mind of the loving Father from all eternity, we have what we call the creation, in time, of a new human person — made for a mighty role on Earth and possibly near Earth as a space man, and certainly for an eternal role with God or without Him, if the person so chooses in life.

So we all have mighty roles as members of God's staff. And it is utterly important to realize this. I concur wholly with Dr. Marra and those who say that there's nothing accidental about creation, except some of the incidents which are within the probabilities of variability due to natural forces (e.g., with earthquake), and of course with human error. But there's no question in my mind as a scientist of thirty years of experience, that this Magnificent, Absolute, Perfect, Omniscient, Omnipotent, Majestic God exists and reigns.

We have been given these responsibilities in our time, in our society, in our place, for a short period, to sustain, to repair, and to further beautify the world of God that we inherit, to "fill God's copy-book" in every respect, theologically, philosophically, morally, physically, chemically, psychologically, artistically, and so on. This is our inheritance. And we can do all of this that God ever delegated to us, perfectly, if we will but ask Him to give us the generous help that He's waiting beside us at all times to give. But God is a gentle Host for the members of His household on this Earth. He never forces His presence upon them, He's always beside us, waiting in anticipation that we will ask Him just for a little more of the help that we need to achieve the greatness, to come up to the hopes that He has for us, that we will rise higher and higher toward that wonderful objective which He has for us, which His Church urges upon us, to be a wonderful, practical, Catholic saint!

Now this period of each person on Earth is set by God, not by man. In this again, the human life issues are of course critical. It's not man's prerogative to call himself into existence, or to call others into existence:

it's God's. Man may initiate the possibility, but man cannot complete the conception. Only God completes a conception, if He concurs with the possibility which the human couple offers Him, should He at that time and place, for His reasons, will that a conception should be completed.

And we will finally be called into God's office usually — in the past — at His instigation, but increasingly in the future, not at His instigation, but at the instigation of man: Man will send us to God through anti-life policies. We will be given our Final Judgment, really a review of the terms of our appointment and our performance under the appointment. To His staff members in God's crew, when He calls us into His office, we have to be ready to answer for our accountability, for our stewardship. And we will either finally be promoted to fully share His court for all eternity; or we will be demoted to be without Him for all eternity, depending upon what we will have earned in justice under His mercy during our life.

Out of pure love, God who needs no one and no thing to complete His Being, has decided to share His attributes, through the creation of beings such as angels, men, the brute animals, the plants, the microbes, the viruses, the inanimate matter, ranging from the purely spiritual to the solely material, which proudly reflect the totality of His Eternal Perfection. Infinity made Himself partly comprehensible to us, by showing us very clearly in many ways what the finite was.

Man Alone Has Been Given These Gifts

Man alone has been given true intellect and true free will, plus major responsibilities for the proper exercise of these faculties on behalf of God – as a resident co-creator and co-manager under God's appointment of Earth, of the particular regions and activities with which he is concerned in his life, with which he should be concerned, the social order, for instance, and whatever parts of the universe man might be allowed to have access to by God. We're only allowed to have access to other parts of the universe beyond the surface of the Earth, under special constraints. We must put on special protective atmospheres to go up even in a jet, to come here. We have to put ourselves in a little protective cocoon otherwise we can't jet from Winnipeg to this place. If we go much higher than 10,000 feet we have to go under pressurization, otherwise we will explode. See, God does not allow anyone to break even a principle of physics two miles above the Earth. Instant death can result, if we defy His physical laws. Any man who goes into the space program and leaves a leak or a bad piece of stitching in his spacesuit will die, like the Russians died due to a leaky door. Three men in the Cosmos program died on their way back because someone made a faulty gasket for their door. Physics is ruthless. It seems that Earth and atmospheres like that around Earth are the only places in creation where the forbearance of God was ever intended to be applied.

Of the many millions of species, with living, material bodies, man alone has the high spiritual nature or soul, which God alone can make and God alone can infuse. What a great unique, marvelous privilege for us! It's a special gift which we alone have, and that's what distinguishes us from the beasts, and that's what makes all the difference, for instance, in sexual matters. All this mating technology that we're getting in our schools, churches, and so on is unnecessary and debasing. The beasts don't need mating technology. It's instinctive, even in humans. To say we need instruction in sexual mechanics, under the guise of sex education is ridiculous. No amount of sexual information can ever substitute for a chronic lack of character formation. Physiochemical means can never solve moral problems! The moral order applies only to humans, in time, because they alone are being steadily created by God, with their unique immortal souls.

The soul of man determines what marriage for the human is all about. It's not a pair of lions teaming up in a cave to have some cubs. Even the lions have better morals than many of our humans today and show much more "marital fidelity." And the beasts are not supposed to know any better. We are. That's what makes the difference, that's really the hinge-pin of all our ideas about sexual matters in relation to humans — the fact that man has a spiritual, unique soul, given from God, in the image of God.

We are temples of the Holy Ghost, and therefore that shows what's wrong with all this fornication, concubinage, pornography and other sexual decadence. Of all creatures, man alone has been given the power to understand, and to decide actions about ultimate issues. Few realize the awesome responsibilities which such faculties of mind and will entail for all of us, once we reach the age of reason. As people increase their knowledge of God's truths, namely reality in all its forms, their power to decide on actions, and their duty to choose morally and wisely in each instance, both increase rapidly, to great heights. If you're worried about handling responsibility, you'd better stop learning. Gathering knowledge is the most dangerous thing a weak person can do, because as he grows in knowledge, he grows in accountability before God for his responsibilities, which he automatically incurs increasingly as his or her knowledge increases.

To meet this challenge, all of us must first acquire the knowledge, the skills, and the virtuous habits essential to managing ourselves properly. And that's what I'm using today instead of the word "discipline." "Self-management" is the term. Don't use discipline, it's an "out" word. Use "management" and it's an "in" word. It's the same concept. Because as Aristotle said, unless you can manage yourself, you cannot manage anything outside yourself. And that's what the Church has always said too. All renewal begins with self-renewal. So let's use that term. We must do these things, manage ourselves well, before we can hope to manage factors outside ourselves. Our poor, sad, chaotic world today urgently needs to learn that very simple lesson.

Dr. Marra has given an excellent introduction to what the Church, particularly through the Popes and St. Augustine, has said about Christian Marriage. There's no need for me to go further into that. The Church has always said that marriage is from God and that the family is the basic cell of society. The family is there for the protection and the perfection of the person, for the generation of new persons, and for the perfection of communities, beginning with the first community which is the family. The Church has always taught these truths, as Vatican II has said in *Gaudium et Spes*: "Authentic married love is caught up into Divine Love, and is governed and enriched by Christ's redeeming power in the saving activity of the Church. Thus this love can lead the spouses to God with powerful effect, and can aid and strenghten them in the sublime office of being a father or a mother." As Dr. Marra and others, particularly von Hildebrand teach and in *Humanae Vitae*, the Holy Father, of course, reminded us as the Church does repetitively, of these essentials.

This is what the Holy Father said about marriage: "Marriage is far from being the effect of chance or the result of the blind evolution of natural forces. It is in reality the wise and provident institution of God the Creator, Whose purpose was to establish in man His loving design." For the husband and wife, that "mutual gift of themselves," and this is again to be emphasized, it's the gift, the self-donation, as von Hildebrand says, "the total self-donation of a couple," is the essence of a marriage. And then out of that should come the sexual relationships, in purity, with love. And out of that, if God so wills to bless them, will come the special fruits of marriage, which are the lovely children: the most priceless, the most marvelous living things in time, below the angels. And that's what the family is, in the Catholic view.

The Flowering of Love: Children

"Love is above all fully human," continues Vatican II, "a compound of sense and spirit. There is love which is total, a very special form of personal friendship: there is love which is faithful and exclusive of all other; and there is love which is fruitful." And that's what the Church essentially teaches: The true flowering of marriage is creative of life. It is somewhat analogous to the true flowering of a beautiful plant in the garden. We put the seeds in, we wait for the growth period, and we finally see the buds come. Then there's the fertilization, and then there are the beautiful lush fruits, such as the lovely tree of peaches. It is a beautiful analogy, which God puts all around us in the citrus trees or the cherries or anything else, to teach us all the time. In effect, He says: "If I intend My fruit trees to be so beautifully and artistically fruitful, and to be delectable, so wonderful, and so beneficial, how much more must I expect men and women to be fruitful, as co-creators with Me?"

If God takes special pains to teach us through His trees and His flowers, and His cats and His dogs, the virtue of generous fruitfulness in the fulfillment of a given nature, for the functions which God intended it, how much more is God trying to teach us, the way He always tries to teach, by every medium. You see, God is the original, perfect media specialist. God knows and teaches everything: God teaches by every means. If He can't get to us through the mind directly, well then, He'll get to us through the heart. Or He'll get to us through the senses, if He can't get to us through the heart as He does to the poor people today who are going down to the edge of Hell on drugs, marital disorder, and semi-suicide. As they're just about to jump over the last brink, they turn and see God's sweet face. God teaches and helps us by every means.

What are children in God's plan? The offspring of a marriage are the normal fruits in a natural sense, but above all, through the natural fruition of a marriage there is a supernatural fruition and completion, and glorification for all eternity of a marriage. The generation of children, then, should normally arise in marriage, barring any unfortunate circumstances, such as illness or other defects of nature; marriages should normally be fruitful. And from this will come the obligation of tending the child.

The first obligation, of course, is to tend the child in the womb. The mother is, above all, God's special appointee to give her body tissues, plus half her genes forever, uniquely, to this new person, whom God has actualized through the soul which He donated, to the receptive cell which the parents generated. And from this moment the mother is honored by God to be the special mother, in a sense that she does something that no one other person can do. She gives the child protection, sustenance, nutrition, waste management services, and so on within her body. And finally, of course, she gives the child birth.

And then she is expected to give the child all the essentials of good care. She's especially appointed by God to be the nurse for that person during his or her formative years. She's especially appointed by God to inculcate with the help of the father into her children all the loving virtues, to give them Christian education, to teach those children all the things they should know in a normal secular sense, with the help of others whom they may subcontract to assist them in these great duties. But remember, the parents are still the primary educators under God. Anybody else, including Bishops, are only to be educating children in the matters of importance in religion, for instance, in doctrine and morals, with the approval of the parents. The parents can delegate others to carry part of their load in teaching, but no one can justly usurp the role of a parent in teaching. And that's what you want to tell the people who are trying to impose sex education and all the other poisonous catechetical junk on our children. The Church and reason say that you can command a Bishop or teacher or anyone else who may be responsible for such evil programs to leave your child alone. We have a duty to tell them to be gone from any such influence over our children.

Responsible Parenthood

What does responsible parenthood mean? Couples must so manage their individual lives in full openness to the will of God, which they cannot foresee, and that's something you must remember at all times. In the light of their circumstances, moderation in all things, including marriage relations, is necessary. Anticipation should precede possession of all things. There is greater joy in anticipation than there usually is in possession, of most factors in life.

And for maximum overall benefits of their marriage, they must never forget that in giving each other to each other, they are expressing a God-given precious option in the eyes of God, in the presence of God, and they are doing so with the blessing of God! In effect, they are lifting up the "hotline phone" to His desk. He must always be left the option of answering this phone, if He so wills. This is the essential message of

Humanae Vitae, issued in 1968. That God is God and God is the Creator of the universe, and that no one less than God can dare to stop, or try to stop, Him being God the Creator!

That's what the Holy Father was inspired by God to write. The Pope is God's only personal direct representative in time, on this Earth now. Like Moses with the tablets, Pope Paul was inspired to proclaim God's reminder of His role in creation, of the priceless value of human life, and of His grave warning to all mankind to promptly cease their anti-God, anti-human life habits. He did this knowing full well that he would be hated, despised, and mocked, as any true man of God must be today. And he delivered a solemn proclamation, an apocalyptic message from God – the significance of which becomes ever more telling every day now, as the anti-life leviathan rolls on at increasing momentum – saying in effect to us all, "God tells me to give you all this message: 'I am still God. And I will not tolerate much longer the notion that man can stop Me being God, that man can determine the existence, and lifespan of My people, in defiance of My will' " in hundreds of millions of cases annually as is taking place through pre- and post-conceptive sins.

Contraception is equivalent to cutting the "hotline" to God the Creator, before He's had a chance to answer it. Then all the subsequent, anti-God, anti-human life sins (which are but the normal fruits of the contraceptive mentality), which are called abortion, infanticide, euthanasia, genocide, and so on, are all but expressions of one act, of one sin, which is slamming the above "phone" down in the face of the Creator, after He has answered it! I believe the latter sins, even though utterly evil, are less so than is contraception, because contraception mocks God's magnificent offer of Life in Himself, to the fruits of human love, when He creates children in cooperation with those parents whom He wishes to honor so highly.

In this context, it is easy to see why the marriage act must always be left open to the will of God. Man freely opts to avail himself of the great privilege of calling upon God to possibly co-create new persons with human assistance; it is *we* who lift up the "phone" to God's desk. Therefore, we must leave to Him the decision as to how He will respond and then graciously accept His decision, the responsibilities, and great opportunities for good in time and for eternity that must be involved for all concerned.

Contraception prevents even the existence of vast numbers of persons intended by God, to help Him and us, to better manage the world, and then to hopefully enjoy the Beatific Vision with Him, for all eternity. All the post-conceptive sins against human life only, in effect, reduce the natural lifespan of the victims, which God had allocated to them; it may have been much longer than the abortionist or euthanasiast would have allowed; but it may not have been. God alone can ever know, and so we must not try to run His business in such matters. But despite the grave sins against God and man involved in the post-conceptive sins, the victims remain eligible to share in His grace and His mercy, in eternity with God. Thus while these acts can, and usually do involve mortal sins, they seem to me to be not half the monstrous sin that contraception or pre-sterilization is. It is a tragic shame that so many otherwise good people cannot adequately appreciate the depths of evil that are inherent to, and which necessarily, sequentially, follow in "mushroom cloud" fashion, and largely irreversibly, from the primary pre-conceptive sins.

As God Leaves the Stage...

God respects man's decision to ask Him to leave the stage of life, and as He leaves the podium, Satan takes over the puppet show that is left, even though the players and most of the audience are oblivious to his presence. From the sidelines, God sorrowfully views the tragic Faustian drama, whose end He knows, as it unfolds; of the children of God making a Hell on earth for themselves, through all the deadly sins derived from pride, and massively expressed through widespread, unending pitiless warfare of a dozen kinds; the loss of the will to govern, except among totalitarians; and among the masses, the concurrent refusal to be governed by anyone; with countless mindless millions expecting instant gratification of their every whim, without restraint or cost to them in any way.

In time, we can never know the will of God in detail, with respect to any person in His creative plan. No one can foretell the destiny of another, because God alone can know it. That's why all the eugenics, all the pre-screening of fetuses, all the abortion, and all the post-birth slaughtering of innocent people through euthanasia, under the euphemism *quality of life*, must stop. God does with humans what He does in the mineral world. He puts His "diamonds" of people usually in shabby, sick, neurally impaired, or otherwise partly imperfect bodies, just as He hides His diamonds, and other gem stones, in the soot cones, or the lava beds spewed out by the volcanoes. He downgrades outer physical appearances and other superficial characteristics, and emphasizes the metaphysical and spiritual factors. For example, poor old Beethoven, born of a syphilitic father and a tubercular mother. We all know of many such cases, such as Helen Keller, Brahms, Berlioz, Pope John XXIII, and the like. God is a master of paradox! Like Him, we must concentrate on the deeper things, in our dealings with our families and our neighbors, trusting in His loving providence to help us all overcome any difficulties which we may encounter during life with mutual charity.

What is God's way of creating people? God creates human persons in two ways, the somewhat routine way and a special way. The somewhat routine way is according to His mathematical probabilities, when the odds on conception are high, should the couple elect union, and He just takes an active interest in each case, and blesses the act. This supplies the basic staffing of the universe, in time. But in a special manner, He creates the special people. It wasn't any accident that Mr. and Mrs. Montini, the peasant couple in Italy, were given little Giovanni who would become Paul VI. Pope Paul was born then, just to do what he's done so well today. God gave that humble couple one of the great Popes of history. It wasn't an accident that Churchill was born 63 years before the Battle of Britain. There was nobody else in the world to carry Churchill's responsibilities. Thus God has special plans for all of us, when He creates us, and we should never forget that.

The fact that man can never foresee God's will in these matters rules out completely all notions of the legitimacy of eugenic "culling" of humans or of their deliberate production by "controlled breeding" practices, as is normal in animal husbandry; and of the possible legitimacy of pre-sterilization or contraception, abortion, infanticide, euthanasia, genocide, and so on. It is an absolutely compelling reason. All anti-human life policies must go, simply because no other person can ever foretell the future, in relation to the destiny of another person.

Contraception is, of course, the initial expression of the satanic attack upon the person and the family. The sequence of anti-God, anti-human life sins that flow from the contraceptive mentality may be illustrated by the chandelier above us today in this room, when inverted. Then the little black knob at its apex would be contraception. To the unwary, it seems to be of small significance. Below it would hang the first conical layer of beads, about one foot high and two feet wide. This could be imagined to represent the voluminous, necessary, first by-product of the contraceptive mentality, which is mass abortions, under a series of high-sounding alibis. Next the layer, much wider and deeper, of very much greater volume, encompassing many more sections of the born human family, as compared to the pre-born babies under attack from abortion, would represent those threatened now by infanticide-euthanasia. Finally, the last layer of the ever widening, deepening cone of vastly greater volume, represents the threat of genocide to all mankind.

When a rock is thrown into a beautiful, tranquil pond (representing God's creation), the waves so formed soon expand outwards concentrically and irreversibly, in the natural order of events. Similarly, as soon as man commits the first of the above series of interdependent sins, namely contraception or pre-sterilization, he breaks the First Commandment; he breaks the delicate lifeline between God and man, in the continuing creation of human persons. The linchpin of the chandelier is broken! Then everything that depended utterly upon this connecting link, such as respect for humans at all stages and all times in life by other humans, collapses as is now obvious.

Once the First Commandment has been mocked, the Second one, which rests upon the First, cannot be expected to be upheld for long, as we now know so well, within and beyond the Church. Since the Second Commandment is merely illustrated in several more ways, by the Third to the Tenth Commandments, these latter must also go down in contempt, by those who habitually mock the First.

For example the lives of so many of the mutineers against *Humanae Vitae* show this trend only too clearly. Once the First has been scrapped by simultaneously approving of contraception and denying the Primacy of the Papacy by which God again proclaimed the objective moral norm on this issue, all the doctrines and moral matters that are upheld by the First Commandment must and have collapsed in the lives of such people. All those who are soft on contraception, the anti-*Humanae Vitae* crowd, must be expected to more readily, more frequently, and more irreversibly, break the other dependent Commandments which primarily concern the moral relationships between humans while the First covers man's duties to God.

Breaking Them All

Those who mock God so deeply, as the pro-contraceptionists do, cannot hope to retain, or exercise for long, any appreciable respect for themselves or for other humans. That is the major reason why all their sickening protestations of "luv" for man in their social-action stunts cannot ring true, or be productive of much good. It is but a sad indicator of their desperate need to create a diversionary smokescreen to cover up for awhile their grave sickness in mind and soul. They are on the road to bitter atheism!

Abortion is the breaking of the Fifth Commandment. We cannot hope to uphold the Fifth if we mock the First. Therefore, it is absolutely futile for those who are soft on contraception to expect to hold the line or win on the abortion issue. All those who, while approving of contraception, think they can save the babies through an anti-abortion, pro-life stand are just damn fools! And, understandably, if we have habitual, deliberate, knowing contempt for God, for His Vicar, for His Magisterium, then how can we expect to retain much respect in any way for man or the environment?

Contraception or pre-sterilization is the axle around which the deadly blades of all the anti-human life movements of our day revolve. These movements widen their coverage of the human race and their brutal lethality as the axle gains speed, as it must, until such time as enough good people regain and infuse into our society that great respect for God, the Creator, the Lord of life, and loving Father of all mankind. Thus the fullest, deepest, holiest respect for the proper use of the marital privilege of initiating the possibility of the co-creation of another priceless person with God (obviously only licit within marriage as ordained by God, within the rules laid down by God and conveyed to us by His Magisterium) is essential to the perfection of marriage and of human societies in every way. It is clearly the key to the slowing down and, hopefully in time, of the reversal of the terrible anti-human life leviathan which is now snowballing over us all.

It is so evil and so dangerous to the possibility of us retaining any decency in our society, of much optimism as to the fate of the family, and of the person with the freedom that God bestowed upon him or her, that God decided to alert us, to warn us, and to beseech us, perhaps for the last time in Western Civilization's history through a "tablet to Moses," a very rare type of audio-visual message, given by His wonderful, courageous, holy Vicar just five years ago[editor's note: the encylical *Humanae Vitae* in 1968] that we must all soon recognize Him again as God the Creator, especially in practice, in all matters involving human life. Otherwise, we will soon complete our man-made hell on earth!

The Floodtide of Anti-Life Activity

The anti-God, anti-creation mentality must generate rapidly the anti-man, anti-child, anti-co-creation attitudes now so deeply ingrained in our society. And Christians must realize that adopting anti-co-creation views, must soon openly turn us against God! Atheism is the logical end of the contraceptive mentality! We are, in fact, often doing our utmost to pervert and, finally, to invert the roles assigned to man by God in His plan of creation.

Thus do we now see all around us the floodtide of perversions of the procreative functions of humans, unashamedly, proudly proclaimed and exposed to us all, with complete contempt for the sensitivities of those of us who have higher values in life (e.g., in the bookstands at every public place, such as in this hotel!), brazenly being poured all over good people, and especially their God-given, precious, innocent children (including our Catholic little ones, in many of our local, officially permitted, supposedly "Catholic" programs), by all the very powerful means available today, such as by the major educational media of history, and by – for most of the children of recent decades in the technically developed world – television; usually with the active backing of the secular state in every way.

And to their great shame, and to the sorrow of we parents and of our children, many of our divinely appointed shepherds have now fled from their primary responsibility to protect and otherwise care for those of God's sheep, especially the little lambs who are the special, chosen prey of Satan's wolves today; as these are being left largely free to prowl as they like amongst our people, in many disguises, including attractive clothes made of lamb's wool! Some of the shepherds have even gone so far as to urge the lambs to fulfill themselves, to show their modern maturity, to find their identity, to grow as persons, by going *out* of the Catholic fold and pasture, under or over the safety fence of God's Magisterium directed by His chief shepherd, our Most Holy Father.

God has obviously generously blessed and sustained Pope Paul all his life, especially during the last decade when, almost alone, this aged, sickly priest of fifty years' great service, this intrepid Bishop and diplomat, this mighty scholar has led us. I was honored to be only a few yards away from His Holiness when, at the audience celebrating the fiftieth anniversary of his ordination, during Pentecost week in May of 1970 in St. Peter's Basilica, he urged us most sincerely, inspiringly, in eight different major languages: "The hour is now striking on the clock of history, which demands great courage from all the Church's children and, in a very special way, the courage of truth. Let your yes, be *Yes*! and your no, *No*! — words Christ enjoined on His disciples of all ages!" How very much better the affairs of Church and State would now be if only just a few more of the Pope's subordinate staff, the cardinals, bishops, priests and nuns, who are accountable to God through him, and we laypeople, Christ's flock, would but follow the Holy Father's fine example as a shepherd!

Pope Paul is a wonderful person who has, and practices, the deepest love for God and for all His children, especially the little ones, from before they can be conceived right through until they return to their Creator for all eternity. I witnessed Pope Paul's great love of and joy with children when, at his anniversary audience, he left his escorting officials to lose himself amongst groups of children, many of them handicapped, to chat with them in their own tongues as he acted as a gentle loving father to them. And there was no doubt that they loved *Il Papa* very much too! Like his Divine Master, grand Pope Paul is saying constantly, clearly, emphatically, by word and deed, "Suffer the little children to come unto Me, for such is the Kingdom of Heaven ... unless you become as little children, you shall not enter the Kingdom."

And his message is the will of God for all of us to heed promptly and fully, as if we were the first Apostles hearing it for the first time from God the Son Himself! He is saying and doing what Christ Himself would say and do today, were He still physically amongst us at this Forum as one of the speakers! Almost alone now, Pope Paul is the torchbearer for human life against all its satanic foes as he bravely stands up, somewhat like the statue of Christ over the Andes Mountains, shining in the dark night for everyone to see, proclaiming the eternal truths of mighty, awesome, and potentially terrible significance for wicked man: that God is still the Creator, especially of continuing human life; that His prerogatives in the creation of new persons of priceless value, and then in deciding their lifespans and possible roles on His team, must be soon again deeply respected by all mankind; and especially that His holy innocents, His children, must be deeply loved, protected, sustained, and helped to the fullest in every way, to achieve the destinies He has willed for all of them individually.

What an example Pope Paul has set us, and how proud we ought to be, in a Catholic sense, to have him now as our chief shepherd, to lead all mankind as God has commissioned and helped him to do; to show up, by sickening contrast, all the hirelings who have fled from their key posts in Church and State after throwing away the means which God gave them to use against the wolves, vixens, crows, and snakes who might dare to come near the flocks, especially the lambs, His children. Some have even persuaded the sheep and lambs to be adventurous enough to go forth in a fine pluralistic way, to join in an ecumaniacal dialogue with the predators, with the sad results now obvious to all of us which were quite predictable.

To be responsible for the abortion of the body of even one of God's holy, innocent children is bad enough. To be accountable to God for large numbers of abortions (e.g., as is Governor Nelson Rockefeller, when by his veto he condemned about 250,000 babies each year now to death, legally, mostly at taxpayers' expense in New York [1973]) is far worse. But to be responsible for the destruction of even one *soul*, of one little born child's spiritual and moral destiny, to be accountable for directing, by omission or commission, one child away from God in time, and for all eternity, instead of back to Him, is an infinitely greater crime and sin which should make every bishop, pastor, religious, and layman (especially we parents) shudder.

That is why we must do our utmost to clean out the polluted, toxic catechetics, sex education, "ratomorphic" psychology, the various species of evolutionism, existentialism, situation ethics, and other anti-rational, anti-God, anti-Catholic, anti-human diseases which have lately flowered in the flock of Christ and beyond, to induce in our society its terminal illness. Thus the obligation upon Catholics, rising rapidly with rank in the Church and State, and upon all men of good will, is to concentrate in practice firstly upon protecting God's right to create His children as He sees fit; and then to attend primarily to the spiritual and moral education of those precious little lambs. God obviously is no Liberal Democrat in important matters, and we are expected to emulate Him in this as in all other issues! As Christ, He put the whips to the new theologians of the very early Church, and scattered their costly, largely parasitic, clerical and business bureaucracies with great gusto, as Catholics worthy of the name should also do now. I believe the first duty of our shepherds of all ranks is now to concentrate upon teaching the Holy Roman Catholic Faith themselves, and through their employees, particularly to our children, as God and His Vicar have so strongly and repeatedly commanded them to do. Otherwise, they should resign, or be fired!

Prophetic Words

God cannot deny to mankind the free will which He gave. Thus the implementation of the will of God, as regards the creation since Adam, of a particular person through human conception then, hopefully, to birth and normal development to full maturity in every way, including spiritually and morally, utterly depends on the cooperation of the parents; then of others who must assist the parents when necessary (e.g., doctors, nurses, bishops, pastors, nuns, and laypeople) at the various stages of existence and development and adversity, of each one of God's children on His behalf. Thus the mighty drama of God's continuing creation largely revolves around the genesis of new children in time.

Now that the anti-child spirit is so widely and deeply ingrained in so high a proportion of the world's potential parents, especially in the technically developed countries, an ever greater responsibility – more than ever before in history – devolves upon those potential parents who still love and respect God and His will, particularly Catholics, and other men and women of good will to be more generously cooperative with God where the possible generation, and then the sustenance, of human life is concerned. Never before did the world have a greater need for Christian flowers in God's garden! Above all, should we decide to avail ourselves, within marriage only, of the special ritual whereby the complete fusion of two persons takes place, in mutual self-donation, to then ascend to the heights of becoming sacral, potential co-creators with God of another child made in the image of God, then obviously we must always leave the act open to the transmission of human life as our Holy Father stressed so strongly in *Humanae Vitae*, in conformity to the teaching of reason, natural law, and of God's Magisterium all through history. It cannot be otherwise if order in creation is to remain where humans are concerned.

When man ignores or, more likely, actively opposes the will of God in these matters, then the Almighty Creator is locally reduced to accepting the miniscule vision of creation, of fallen, sinful human couples as to who shall be conceived, born, and allowed the opportunity to work alongside God at their assigned tasks during life and then to spend eternity with or without Him. The very essence of the creative process in geographical, temporal, then eternal terms is deeply and, in such cases, irreversibly inverted — the lowly creature in mortal sin runs the local human scene through perverting the major role of the primary cell of society, the family.

But God is not mocked by man for long, anywhere, anytime. When a group of humans sets out to defy Him, especially in the co-creation of His children, for His purposes, for His reasons, far beyond the particular understanding of any potential parents at the time, then God calls into action His contingency plans to ensure the adequate staffing of His Church and of His world, as His love, His promise, and His providence requires. He gives extra blessings to those parents who still respect His will, including in the form of more children than He had earlier intended to offer them, to compensate for the many potential parents elsewhere who have decided to mock His generosity when offered to them. He has already done this in the case of countries such as Poland, Africa (as Bishop Okoye from Nigeria, can readily confirm), India, South America, and elsewhere among the materially poorer countries, where Our Lord is quite at home with His people — in foreknowledge of the present mood in the affluent countries. He has made great, more than adequate, plans to serve us and our children with His bishops, priests, and Religious, in unpolluted condition from these countries, as those of such vocations from our countries and from

Ireland disappear as they must as the spirit of pride, rather than that of absolutely vital humility with sanctity, has come to dominate most of the candidates for such offices, and especially infected institutions in which they are being prepared for their sacred tasks.

Most of our Western world seminaries are so badly polluted that simple sanitation procedures will never be sufficient to clean them up again to a point where we could again urge our children to offer themselves to them, to prepare well to serve God and man. Rather, like a pathogenically infected body, they will have to be quarantined and then buried deep in history. This is already well under way, thanks be to God!

It is interesting to note how, in God's providence, poverty has largely protected the poor countries from being polluted by the current revivals of the ancient errors which have plagued the Church all through history. The Rhine region is like a barnyard that is permanently infected with toadstools of every kind, including attractive theological and moral ones. As the environment cycles, they regularly pop up into the daylight, when conditions are favorable (e.g., as they have been during recent decades). And, of course, many amateur pilgrims, just out of our modern schools of ignorance, anti-reason, and self-deception, in a psychedelic state, feast unsuspectingly on these attractive morsels to their great but quite predictable sorrow.

Through poverty, God has largely prevented the diseases which today so threaten the Church in the United States, in Canada, and in the rest of the Western countries from being spread to the poorer lands. Fortunately, these poorer lands could not afford to send their best young men and women overseas to become infected from our corrupting ex-Catholic universities, seminaries, and convents. Nor could they afford to subscribe to all the polluted books, journals, papers, and liturgical-catechetical toadstools, nor build up the large, parasitic bureaucracies, the operating arm of the counter-Catholic Magisterium, which have wrought such havoc to us and to our Church, especially our children, God's little precious lambs, given to our care for a short time. Nor can they offer the high fees and high living which are normally required to entice the major polluters (speakers and teachers) to come to their poor, often unpleasant, countries.

Now we are beginning to see the unfolding of God's staffing plan for the white, affluent countries. Since so many of our people have declined God's offer of His children in favor of pet fish, cats, dogs, and motorized animals like Mustangs (there are about 750 million pets in the USA, with three times as many vehicles, five times as many dogs, and eight times as many cats, born every minute now here, as there are babies born! [1973]) God has obviously given many of the souls He intended to infuse into white bodies – to fill our seminaries and convents, hospitals, schools, etc., the way they are filled now in Nigeria and elsewhere in the poor lands overseas – to cooperative parents with darker skins. The final irony is now coming, when in order to have a really Catholic young priest or nun at our side when needed, especially for our children's needs in catechetics, morals, and spirituality, we will have to import them at our expense and to the benefit of the overseas sources of them (which desperately need financial support to cope with the large numbers, beyond their possible local needs), yes, *import* fine young people offering their lives to serve God and man, just when and where they will be so much needed. And for white people to have to actually depend on darker-skinned, holy, servants of God, for their spiritual and temporal support in their greatest needs, should do vast additional good. Several countries are now beginning to take over the great, recent role of Ireland, including no doubt to supply missionaries to Ireland soon!

The foregoing gives one some idea of the immense, unique privileges which God bestows upon those parents, shepherds, pastors, nuns, brothers, and laypeople, who coordinate their wills with His as regards the creation, protection, and support of His wonderful children all through life and beyond. His endless gratitude, and that of the children who grow in His grace, are assured to all who act in such a manner. That should be a great source of consolation to us all, when difficulties come our way when children are involved. Correspondingly, woe to those who do not act as God requires them to act in relation to His little ones!

The Unique Privilege of Parenthood

With regard to the unique privilege given by God to us as parents, I want to emphasize a couple of points. The first thing is, when God picks spiritual parents, the Bishops, the Popes, the priests, the sisters, and other celibates in the holy life, He says to them: "God bless you for offering to give up your physical generative powers to make humans of your own genes, to be in Heaven with you and Me; and instead, you make spiritual children with Me." That's what we mean by celibacy. That's what we mean by total dedication, total sublimation of the sexual potential of the person to the will of God. That's why celibacy must never be given up as the ideal of the priesthood and of the religious life.

The next point concerns the laymen, and especially married people — some of the things that God gives us to do, for example, the mighty roles we have in partnership with Him. For instance, we have under God the privilege of generating all God's workers in creation in time, and some very special ones. We alone can conceive, bear, and rear the future popes, bishops, priests, nuns, and layworkers for God. That's the laymen's privilege, God bless us. Let's stay with Christian parenthood, let's never downgrade it. In the physical order, we have duties which are tremendous for managing the universe. God says, "My resources are ample — manage them well for Me!" And I fully agree with God. We have five times enough food for all human numbers now, the pollution story is totally unnecessary; we can clean this world up while we have more people than ever, and busier than ever. Put a vacuum cleaner over the home, the more you use it the more you clean the home up. That's what I do in my work: clean a little of the world up.

Then, of course, just think what parenthood means in the family sense. We have a desire and obligation to stay deeply together. On Earth, of course, that means we must cement the whole family together strongly in every possible way, both personally and in groups. We have a Wanderer family here, and a Christian family right through history, the communion of saints, and so on, so that all of us will eventually join God again and our friends for all eternity in Heaven.

And of course, we have the example, the Holy Family itself. They are exemplars in each case for all of us individuals. Christ Himself became a perfect human baby, child, teenager, and adult, to show that it could be done. Mary, the supreme Woman, the Mother of God, the Mother of us, the Protectress of the Church, the Queen of creation, including Heaven, absolutely refused to set up women's lib. She knew better! She was the ideal of the mother and the girl. She knew the differences between *vive la difference* and discrimination. There's nothing wrong with respecting differentiation, when it's naturally so. Discrimination is causing a difference where one doesn't exist by nature.

The last stage of the Holy Family, the death of Christ, visually portrays what we foresee coming for us. Our Lady was with her Divine Baby and Son. He was a perfect Son all His life, a perfect young man, a perfect teenager. His beloved loyal Bishop-elect, St. John, was there. Eleven-twelfths of the Bishops-elect skipped, including the first Pope-elect. Things have not become worse, they've improved — we have the Pope also with us today, thank God!

So, above all, we have the Holy Father and Our Lady with us. If any of us have any doubts on what Christian Marriage is all about, and have difficulties in Christian Marriage which must be faced, we must go back to Our Lady, above all, and tell her about it; then ask her to tell her Son about it; and from that little dialogue, I'm sure they'll solve it for us. And then in time, they'll give us all the help we need to bear it, such that, when finally God calls us (or man sends us to Heaven — and a lot of us are going to be sent, don't worry), we will get the greatest, most exhilarating surprise in our whole life, to be met by a welcoming committee of the Holy Family.

Dr. Reginald Gallop delivered this address at the Ninth National Wanderer Forum. Dr. Gallop founded and for several years directed the Food Science Department at the University of Manitoba in Winnipeg. A native of Sydney, Australia, he graduated in organic chemistry and worked with the Commonwealth Scientific and Industrial Research Organization. He worked in the integration of specialized knowledge toward the production and distribution of foods for man and livestock on a world basis and toward the elimination of pollution problems. Through his work with food production, Dr. Gallop became an expert on population problems, and became convinced the "problem" does not exist.

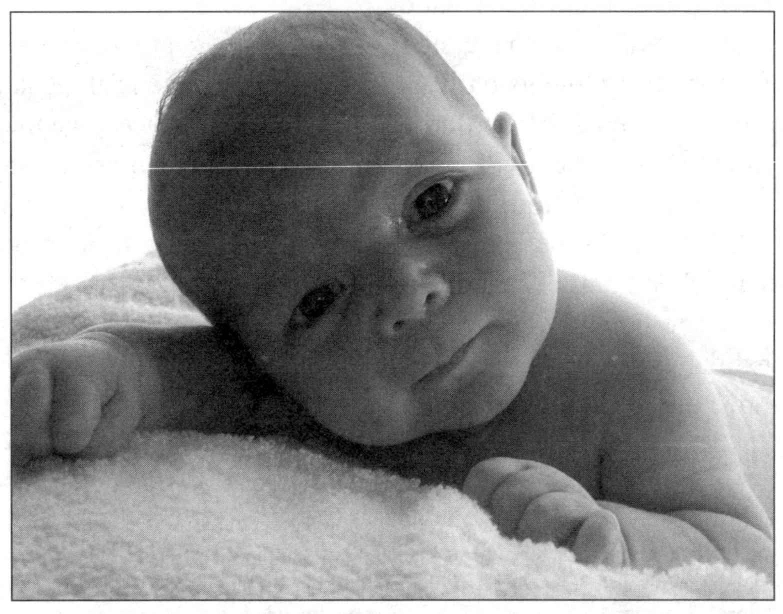

To be responsible for the abortion of even one of God's holy, innocent children is bad enough.... To be responsible for the destruction of even one soul is an infinitely greater crime.

—Photo by Nicole Paslawski

A SIGN OF CONTRADICTION

William H. Marshner
Washington, D.C.

The sign of contradiction: we all know what *that* is, don't we? It is the encyclical *Humanae Vitae* [Pope Paul VI, 1968]. Now, I want to begin with the fact that *Humanae Vitae is* a sign of contradiction; a sign of contradiction, however, to what? I suggest that it is a contradiction to the modern world at something terribly central to that world.

As a starting point, I wish to suggest that 400 years ago, Western man launched himself upon an adventure that was ambiguous at its very core. On the one hand, Christian man would shatter the frontiers of the known world. He could crack open the ptolemaic universe like an egg; he would hurl himself with banners of Christ the King onto a thousand shores where that banner had never been planted before. And on the home soil of Europe, Christian man, freed from the paralyzing grip of cosmological mythology, would penetrate the secrets of nature, to lay bare the answers that would deliver man from the ancient scourges of disease, hunger, and poverty.

But on the other hand, modern man would seek more than liberation from scourges. He would seek also another kind of liberation; and in this case, he would seek liberation from nature itself. Science, become demiurgical, would be at the service of mere will to dominate nature and create through the domination of nature a new Eden. Not the paradise of God but the paradise of sin — the paradise in which all nature and all nature's energy is at the service of mere human will, so that by exercise of that will, though it be a sin, man is safe, fortified by his domination of energy. To construct a paradise of sin, a new Eden from which no angel, no matter how powerful, not even God Himself, could cast man out — that, it seems to me, is the deeply ambiguous project of the modern world.

In pursuing this conquest of nature, man lost sight, I think, of one of the central things which *Humanae Vitae* teaches, and it is just here that *Humanae Vitae* stands in striking contradiction to the project of modernity. *Humanae Vitae* at least insists on this: that at some point in the process of dominating nature, you cease to be dealing with merely neutral facticity. At some point you come up against something within nature itself, within the experienced world itself which is nevertheless normative — something which expresses a deep "ought" written into the very nature of things and which simply cannot be bulldozed away. It was this distinction which modern science and modern philosophy over the course of four hundred years was removing from vision.

Medieval man, it seems to me, was capable of finding deep moral significance in what we would regard as mere matters of facticity; that trees grew and that they were green, that flowers budded in the spring. All these things were diaphonies of God, of His intelligibility, of His design for the universe, to medieval man. But as modern man became practiced in the art of transforming nature, in the art of interfering with mere facts, to make the causal sequences work better according to his will, this diaphony of things disappeared. It was clouded over, and more and more it came to be thought that there was *nothing* in nature which spoke of a deep or God-given necessity. It came to seem as if all nature were merely a system of facts, a system of energy bonds and relationships which could be shuffled, broken, or reconstituted at the pure service of human will. There was a loss of a sense of something normative in things, something normative in nature.

A Man-Made Crisis

Now as nature became meaningless to man, the crisis of modernity began to set in, did it not? Previously, we could at least say that all nature as a system had this much meaning to it: namely that it cradled and sustained man. There was a relationship between the environment and man, whereby environment was the support and man the supported. But the triumph of technology had done away with that relationship, in fact reversed it one hundred percent. Today it depends upon us to worry about the oil slicks and upon us to save the baby seals and upon us not to press the button which will incinerate the world. Today it is the environment which is cradled in man and not man who is cradled in the environment. And we find the situation unlivable! Perhaps we are beginning to rediscover a deep and normative relationship after all. Maybe this is what the ecological crisis is all about.

But there was an earlier sign that something was wrong in modern man's moral exploitation of nature, it seems to me, the first definitive sign, the crucial sign for our time. It was the promulgation of *Casti Connubii* and then the promulgation of *Humanae Vitae*. Here at last man had come up against something with which it was not permitted to tamper.

The well-known Viennese psychiatrist, Viktor Frankl, says that what is most basic in man is a will to meaning, that is to say a basic drive toward intelligibility, an interest in things. Man, Dr. Frankl says, is defined by his intentionality, by the fact that he seeks to know. But when this seeking to know, this will toward meaning is frustrated in man, then he enters into either one of two perversions: either a will to power or a will to pleasure.

Now in our present case, the will to meaning has been frustrated for modern man for 400 years by false metaphysics, by a false understanding of what nature really is. Nature having become opaque and unintelligible, the will to meaning frustrated, then the uses of nature must turn either to sheer power or else to sheer pleasure. In our present case, I believe that many speakers have discussed already what man does with his own biological nature when he succumbs to the will to power. We have discussed, I believe, some of the terrifying aspects of genetic engineering, the manipulation of the race, the construction of a whole new way to misuse human beings. I will not discuss that. I will go on, rather, to what man does when he succumbs to the will to pleasure, in these matters.

As you know, Catholic teaching on the relationship between the sexual act and its ends, the unitive function and the procreative function, is a delicate one. Basically, let's begin this way. The Catholic teaching rejects the proposition unequivocally of sex as sport. And I think that in doing this, it steers between, if you will, a Scylla and a Charybdis. On the one hand, Catholic teaching insists on avoiding the Scylla of a rigorism which could be stated this way: that sexual relations are intrinsically gross and that God, out of a general condescension toward human weakness, concedes to His Church the right to pass a thin veil of respectability over this intrinsically gross business, when and only when it is performed within the bounds of matrimony and even then, only for the sake of procreation. That's Scylla. That is a manifest distortion of Catholic teaching. It was Tertullian's idea by the time he became a Montanist. Earlier he had had better ideas.

But then there is also Charybdis. And I think Charybdis is best expressed for us in a laxist proposition which was condemned by Innocent XI in the year 1679, which reads as follows: *Opus coniugii ob so lam voluptatem exercitum, omni penitus carit culpa ac defectu veniale.* It isn't so bad that it needs to stay in Latin, so I will translate for you. It says: "The marital act, performed solely for the sake of pleasure, lacks almost all guilt or venial defect." How do you like that! That proposition, according to the teaching of the Roman Catholic Church, is a heresy. In other words, the true proposition is that the marital act, indulged in solely for the sake of pleasure, possesses guilt, is culpable, and a matter of venial sin at least. Now that is a truth which is profoundly lost sight of today, but it shows the Charybdis away from which Catholic teaching steers. Whether in matrimony or outside matrimony, it is no good imagining that the sexual act can be used solely for the sake of gratification, that it can be turned into fun and games.

Now what lies between this Scylla and Charybdis? What lies there is the clear channel of Catholic affirmation that sexual union is the incarnation or if you will, the completion of a spousal love, a love which is by nature open to the transmission of life. Now what does that mean? That means that the marriage act may be pursued for the sake of that spousal love and as an incarnation of that love.

Notice the condemned proposition did not say **ob** *solam amorem*, but *ob solam* **voluptatem.** And falling in love is not the same as a joy ride, at least this is my impression of the matter. Love is not *voluptas.* It is *amor.* The marriage act can be done for love without a direct intention to have a child at this moment; and yet what is done for love, if it is a fully open and self-transcending love, is always open to the transmission of life, at least by the refusal to insert some kind of active intervention which will close off the love from that openness toward the transmission of life.

I do not propose at this point to dwell on the distinction between the rhythm method and the false and abominable methods of birth control which are known as artificial contraception. I suspect that you know this teaching quite well. We have already laid the fundamental basis for it: that whereas these other methods close out the sacrificial and indeed penitential aspect which is always part of a genuine love, the rhythm method does not do so; that whereas artificial contraception refuses to recognize within nature a normative and God-given structure which cannot be interfered with, on the other hand the rhythm method precisely presupposes that structure and the intelligent use of that structure as a God-given reality.

I will not pursue that subject. Rather I want to raise the question now, is *Humanae Vitae* infallible? This, it seems to be, is where we begin to get down to the nitty-gritty as we pursue our controversies in the Church at the present time. I am sure everyone at this Forum is an ardent defender of the Catholic Church's teaching in *Humanae Vitae*. The question is, how are we to pursue that argument? How are we to pursue that defense? I would suggest first of all that we have to be absolutely clear in our own minds that the teaching of *Humanae Vitae* is infallible. And we have got to be able to strip away all theological arguments which suggest that it is not infallible, that it's in any way something less than infallible, irreversible, irremediable.

Is *Humanae Vitae* Infallible Teaching?

First of all, I think we can insist, without fear of contradiction, that *Humanae Vitae* represents a teaching of the ordinary Magisterium. But it is a teaching of the ordinary Magisterium which is infallible as such. You can have a doctrine which is infallible through being taught by the ordinary Magisterium. Now what does that mean? It means a doctrine which has been taught always, everywhere, throughout the world, and especially by the Popes in the form of encyclical letters. The ordinary Magisterium is the whole, routine teaching action of the Church apart from unusual interventions in the form of solemn *ex cathedra* definitions. Solemn *ex cathedra* definitions in the history of the Church have always related to matters strictly of Christian revelation. But in the ordinary Magisterium, the Church gets into other areas as well, for example, into areas of natural law. That is what we get into here.

Now the teaching of *Humanae* Vitae is infallible because it is an exact repetition and deepening of the teaching of *Casti Connubii* issued in 1930. And concerning the authority of *Casti Connubii,* I want to quote for you the remark of no less than John T. Noonan, who says as follows:

> "How great was that authority — the authority of *Casti Connubii*? By the ordinary tests used by theologians to determine whether a doctrine is infallibly proclaimed, it may be argued that the specific condemnation of contraceptive interruption of the procreative act is infallibly proclaimed. The encyclical is addressed to the universal Church. The Pope speaks in fulfillment of his Apostolic office, he speaks for the Church. He speaks on moral doctrine that he says 'has been transmitted from the beginning.' He promulgates the teaching. If the Pope did mean to use the full authority to speak *ex cathedra* on morals, which Vatican I recognizes as his," Noonan concludes by asking, "what further language could he have used?"

The same conclusion was reached by Hans Küng in his preface to *Infallible? An Inquiry*. If you recall the argument there, Küng said, look, in 1930, an encyclical is promulgated which reasserts a teaching which had always been there. No Catholic theologian — Noonan also recognizes this some place — no Catholic theologian had ever said that contraception was good or morally permissible. So then along comes an encyclical in 1930 which re-insists on this. It is handed over to all the Bishops of the world. It is dissented from nowhere. And for thirty-eight years, every Bishop in Christendom harps on this, dissents nowhere, and the faithful are told that they must obey this doctrine under pain of damnation. If the idea of an ordinary Magisterium, if the idea of Catholic tradition means anything, then this is a matter of infallible doctrine. This could not possibly be gone back on. To go back on this central doctrine would be to maintain that the Church for thirty years has openly and in the ears of all mankind and in the ears of all her sons and daughters, and through her Popes and through all her bishops, taught a lie. There is simply no way to get out of that. Hans Küng knows it. He says the Roman theologians were right, according to the understanding of the ordinary Magisterium, there is no way to get out of this.

What am I going to do? Küng asks himself. Get rid of the entire magisterial system. Infallible, that's the question mark now!

With the basic contention out of the way, let's get into a couple of the nuances. The theologians, the so-called dissenting theologians are, of course, boundlessly clever in nitpicking and inventing distinctions which no one ever thought of before to find some basis on which to say that the present encyclical, although it repeats what has been always been said, is somehow not to be taken seriously as an infallible teaching. Notice, I insist that the teaching of *Humanae Vitae* is what is infallible. It is entirely independent of the question whether the encyclical is, in form, itself an infallible pronouncement. That is neither here nor there. That is purely a question, it's almost a question of ceremony.

How Dissenters Change Opinion

The first argument which is brought up by the dissenters in order to get themselves a hook out of this, is to argue that the teaching of *Humanae Vitae* is a little different from other things which belong to the ordinary Magisterium because this teaching is a matter of natural law. It is one thing if the ordinary Magisterium has always said that the Holy Spirit proceeds from the Father and Son. That's a matter of revealed doctrine. But when you get into the area of natural law, you are in the area of something which is not the exclusive domain of the Magisterium; rather you're in the area of something which belongs to all mankind to comment upon, because we all have this nature. So Papal authority rests on a different footing when it talks about natural law, according to this argument. And the footing which it rests on, needless to say, is one which allows theologians, in the name of humanity, to dissent because they [think] they have a deeper and richer experience of human nature than the Pope does. Now in order to drive home this comparison a little bit further, they insist on comparing *Humanae Vitae* in its authoritative impact, in its direct, morally binding force on the individual, to the social encyclicals, *Rerum Novarum* or *Quadragesimo Anno* or something of this kind.

Now it is perfectly true that in the social encyclicals, once again, the Church is largely dealing with matters of natural law or matters at least of natural wisdom (the fundamental constitution of the state, the natural order of society). These are not revealed matters. So again there seems to be some superficial merit to this comparison. However, please note, in the social encyclicals the Church is talking about matters largely of analysis. It is analyzing the disease of the modern world. And insofar as these encyclicals propose remedies, they propose remedies which presuppose the cooperation of large numbers of people and institutions, sometimes presupposing an entire reconstruction of the international order, certainly the international monetary order.

In other words, the direct moral obligation on the individual to implement the teaching of a social encyclical is nowhere near as great as the direct moral obligation to implement the teaching of *Humanae Vitae*, because you *can* obey the latter. It only takes two to tango there. That's all. You can do it. Reconstructing the social order may require a few more allies.

Moreover, the Church simply insists that there is no distinction between her right to teach about natural law and her right to teach specifically revealed Christian matters. Rather, for example, in the encyclical *Ubi Arcano* of Pius XI, the Church insists that she alone, and uniquely she, of all the institutions to be found in the world has the sole right of forming consciences about matters public and private, natural and revealed. So in other words, according to the Magisterium's own definitive statements, there is simply no ground for this distinction. We could get into the theological basis for why there ought not be a ground for the distinction. It would, however, take us far afield.

A second argument which is brought up is the argument from changed circumstances. It is a variety of the chronolatry, the notion that history itself has a content, or as Prof. Gallop says, that the clock has an intellect. Changed circumstances. "Well," it is said, you know, "*Casti Connubii*, yes that came out in 1930. Well, it was a different world then, wasn't it? Somehow within the last thirty-eight years — mankind has passed through an enormous psycho-spiritual mutation." (Perhaps a psycho-sexual mutation, I don't know.) "The laws which made sense in 1930, in that world, do not make any sense anymore in our world of today." Now it is always very hard to pin down what happened, and in what year it happened, that made all this change. We are not told. But insofar as any argument is brought forward at all, we are told that, "You see, there is a new social reality." And this new social reality really amounts to the economic needs of the middle class. Since 1930, more and more people have gotten middle class. Now to become middle class is essentially to desire a stereo and a swimming pool. These are expensive things. If you are not middle class, you are content with your wine and spaghetti. You do not care about the swimming pool, you are not all that interested in these things, and so you can afford a child or two. But once you get into the middle class, into the revolution of rising expectations, then children become increasingly hard to put up with, and this is alleged to create a great moral crisis, so that the teaching of the past must be changed.

And here the comparison is made to the teaching on usury. It is alleged, that once upon a time, the structure of society, the presuppositions that men had about economic affairs, were such that the Church's teaching on usury made sense. However, things went through a mutation. People got better economic ideas, they created different structures, and so quietly, without a great deal of fanfare, the Church just swept the whole usury thing under the rug. It is now gone and no longer obliges anyone as a moral teaching.

Well, the trouble with this comparison, unfortunately, is that it's simply not true. The teaching on usury does still bind. But the interesting thing, I think, is that the teaching on usury still makes sense. And on this point, I am astonished to be able to quote John Maynard Keynes in this book, *The General Theory of Employment, Interest, and Money*:

> "I was brought up to believe that the attitude of the medieval Church to the rate of interest was inherently absurd and that the subtle discussions aimed at distinguishing the return on money loans from the return to active investment were merely Jesuitical attempts to find a practical escape from a foolish theory. But I now see these discussions as an honest, intellectual effort to keep separate what the classical theory[he means Smith and Ricardo, et al.] has inextricably confused together, namely, the rate of interest and the marginal efficiency of capital. For it now seems clear that the disquisitions of the schoolmen were directed towards the elucidation of a

formula which should allow the schedule of the marginal efficiency of capital to be high whilst using rule and custom and moral law to keep down the rate of interest."

So you see, the mutation does not work in the case of the example cited. The Church's teaching [on usury] makes sense and is still in force. Neither does it work in the case of *Humanae Vitae*.

Freedom of Conscience

Well, when all things fail and when people get skeptical about the idea that they or their parents went through an enormous psycho-sexual mutation between 1930 and 1968, then one comes down to another argument, namely, freedom of conscience. And here, Vatican II is set against the Pope. It is alleged that the *Declaration on Religious Liberty*, which, by the way, never mentions the term "freedom of conscience," nevertheless somehow prevents the Pope from issuing a teaching which pretends to bind anyone in conscience.

Well, it is sufficient to point out that the *Declaration on Religious Liberty* has nothing to do with any alleged freedom of conscience for a very simple reason. Conscience is not free with respect to the Church's Magisterium. It is only free, and thank God, with respect to the coercion of the State. And that is the point to which the *Declaration on Religious Liberty* is directed. The Declaration insists that the government does not have the right to compel you, for example, to be baptized or to practice a particular religion or to practice no religion. Supreme Court beware. It does not and cannot allege a freedom of conscience with respect to the claims on truth of the Catholic Church, because if it did allege such a religious "liberty of conscience," then the *Declaration on Religious Liberty,* in addition to being intrinsically absurd, would be in flat contradiction to the *Syllabus of Errors*, which proclaims that it is the moral duty of man to seek the unity of the one true Church. So conscience cannot be brought up as a claim here.

And by the way, isn't this argument from conscience just too absurd for words? Whose conscience ever *compelled* him to practice contraception? Nonsense. The most people claim is that "My moral reasoning excuses it." That it is "permitted." The argument is analogous to the one which is used, you know, when they talk about unifying the North and South of Ireland. They say: "Oh my goodness, the poor Protestants. The Catholics are going to impose upon them their morality and their tender consciences will be injured." What is one of the issues in connection with which this argument is brought up? Divorce. "They're going to be forbidden to divorce." As if anybody's conscience ever compelled him to get a divorce. Your conscience can't compel a thing like that. Merely defective moral reasoning can excuse it. The whole issue of conscience here is a phony one.

Finally, the dissenters resort to the argument that theologians have a unique role of input to the work of the Magisterium. The Bishops, to be sure, have their part to play; they hold councils and do the voting, and so forth. But the theologians have a certain positive contribution too, which can be manifested, they say, through responsible dissent. Now this is justified by vague references to collegiality and to co-responsibility. And it is actually alleged that Vatican II creates this new, special role for theologians. The difficulty with this argument is that in the 103, 014 words of the sixteen official documents of Vatican Council II, the theologians are never once mentioned as a separate or special class within the Church.

Failing all else, the dissenters tried to use the press as a novel means to secure a magisterial status. A theological note, if you will. I think this is perhaps the first time in history that something like this has been tried. What they said was this: "The newspapers are full of stories about the Commission in Rome, the rumor mills are very active, and we know for a fact that the teaching on birth control is going to be changed. All right, now if we know for a fact that the teaching is going to be changed, then the law presently in force suddenly has to have a huge question mark behind it. We then resort to the scholastic maxim, *Lex dubia non obligat:* 'A doubtful law does not oblige.' Whereupon the situation is thrown open, and we use the rules of moral probabilism to say that either of two probably moral actions may be pursued." So the door was thrown wide open.

A Time for Action

Now what this argument ignores, in addition to the fact that *Casti Connubii* was in no sense subject to change, is the fact that throughout this entire period the *Pope* was saying, "The teaching is not going to change." He said, "There is no doubt on this doctrine." Remember that? Press conference after press conference, yet only a handful of newspapers reported it. It's as though the Holy Father was deliberately strangled by a press policy in order to create doubt about laws in force in the Church, in order to be able to throw things open and invoke falsely the problematic of moral probabilism. It is just an incredible piece of arrogance even to bring this up as an argument. It is to appeal to your own vicious handiwork as casting doubt on the Church's teaching!

The long and short of it is that the teaching is here. Now what do we do with it? What I suggest is this: We need a twofold approach. And here I come to my peroration. On the one hand, in our attempt to witness to this doctrine, we are dealing with married sinners. We are dealing with people who in some sense want to be Catholics and yet who for one reason on another, practice illicit means of contraception. What do we do with those people? I think we have a beautiful example in *The Wanderer* in recent days. There was a letter from a woman saying she could not accept the teaching, and the replies flowed from *The Wanderer*'s readership, replies which were in every respect touching and compassionate, setting forth the doctrine of the Faith, but in such a way that its beauty was revealed. One had to reconsider one's position. I think that's one way we deal with this thing.

A second way is that if you have a gift for dealing with souls, you may be able to spot behind a moral argument (such as claiming that birth control is licit) the spiritual flaw, the source of pride or whatever, which is urging a person to advance this argument, which is giving the person the self-interest to sustain this argument. You may be able to deal with that. More power to you.

If you are unable to deal with people in that way, then my own experience is that it is better to use a flanking attack. On the level of pure argument, it is very difficult to get anywhere talking about *Humanae Vitae* directly. People will not listen to you. Rather you can do two things, it seems to me. Absolutely insist that the teaching is infallible; get rid of all their attempts to argue that they can somehow still be Catholics and reject it. If you have your theological texts in hand you can prove to these people that the claims to the effect that the encyclical is not infallible are just nonsense. Try to rekindle in them a loyalty to the Catholic Faith, a new respect for the Catholic Faith through another means. And by the grace of God they may well be moved to reconsider their position on this doctrine. If you can convince them, for example, of how right the Church was on abortion, they may go back and reconsider on contraception. The hardened ones won't, but some will. That is my pastoral advice about how to cope with married sinners.

Now, I put that all on one hand, and I'm going to talk about on the other hand: what to do about priests and bishops, official catechists, and people like that who hedge or deny this doctrine. I recommend a policy of absolutely no mercy! I recommend a policy which says, "Yes, *Humanae Vitae* is the sign of contradiction and we are going to make *you* signs of contradiction too, in the light of this sign of contradiction." These people must not be allowed to hide behind ambiguous formulas. If they will not teach clearly and without any equivocation whatsoever the doctrine of the Church, then they must be exposed, they must be called heretics, and they must be driven from their charges.

Now why is this important to do? Well, I suggest that we think for one minute about this problem in an absolutely terrifying theological context. According to the doctrine of St. Thomas, a sinner, somebody in mortal sin, continues to belong to the Mystical Body of Christ, continues to belong to the Church through the supernatural virtue of faith which he still possesses, although it's not formed by charity. It's called unformed faith. He still possesses his faith, which still unites him in a certain way to Christ. But if you commit a sin against the Faith, you lose all. If through unbelief a heretic destroys this faith within himself, he severs his last link with the Mystical Body of Christ, and he ceases to be a member of the Church. According to St. Thomas, the heretic is cut off from the Church, whatever may be his outward behavior, even if through pure hypocrisy he continues to profess in public the faith he has denied in his heart.

Now, an undisclosed heretic could continue to exercise a ministry, a jurisdiction within the Church, of whose nullity he alone was aware. You see what I'm driving at. What an enormous and serious uncertainty could enter into the Church! Now this uncertainty would pertain to all things which are a matter of jurisdiction connected with an office. It does not pertain with those things that go with receipt of the Sacrament of Orders. As we know, an apostate priest can still consecrate, if he has the intent to do so. This is a great and terrifying problem in itself (the case of an ineradicable character). I'm not talking about that. I'm talking about legitimate powers of jurisdiction.

Trust the Holy Spirit

Now how do we resolve this problem? Well, I'll give you a scary answer, and then I'll give you a more reassuring answer. The most detailed treatment on this subject is in the *Summa de Ecclesia* written in 1560 by a theologian named Turrecremata. He said this: that a bishop in such a state of secret heresy loses all jurisdictional power. Now what are we going to do? Turrecremata says : "My hope is this. We are guaranteed by Christ that the things necessary for salvation will never be lacking to the Church. Therefore the Holy Spirit will provide what is necessary, either by permitting the secret heresy to be discovered or by making good somehow what has been left undone in this null jurisdiction." In other words, the main hope, according to his theory, is that the Holy Spirit will allow the secret heresy to get out, so that we will know who has real authority over us in Christ and who does not!

Now I want to leave you in a state of doubt and not a state of terror, because there's a contrary opinion, namely that of Cardinal Journet, who argues in *L'Eglise du Verbe Incarne* that secret heresy does, indeed, exclude a man from the Church but it does not *ipso facto* entail the cessation of his jurisdictional powers.

I just want to leave you with the unpleasant thought that this is an open question in the Church. The theologians differ on this point. We have got to have a strategy which gets at this problem of secret heresy. Maybe in the Providence of God the taking the lid off at Vatican II was directed towards this very end. Who knows what would have been broiling underneath the surface if the situation of the late fifties had gone on any further? But now the heretics are coming out of the carpets. Let us use the sign of contradiction to bring out all the heretics in the carpet!

Dr. William H. Marshner, KHS, delivered this address at the Ninth National Wanderer Forum in St. Paul, Minnesota. Marshner entered his collegiate studies with a view to a career in the Lutheran ministry. He studied at Yale in the field of Near Eastern and Biblical languages and literature and converted to the Catholicism in 1967. The author of books and countless articles on the Faith, Marshner holds a doctorate in sacred theology from the John Paul II Insitute and teaches in the theology department of Christendom College in Front Royal, Virginia.

Beyond Splendor: The Other Side of the Coin

Christopher Derrick
London, England

The subject the Splendor of Christian Marriage, reminds me of the story about a priest who once preached a lofty and eloquent sermon about the splendor of Christian marriage. It was a very fine sermon. And afterwards as the people were leaving the Church, a battered-looking old Irish woman was heard to remark, "Ah, I wish I knew as little about marriage as his reverence does!"

That story touches a nerve in all of us, perhaps not in the celibates among us, but possibly even in them. And we don't need to believe that the woman in the story had necessarily suffered any of the obviously terrible disasters that can come upon a marriage — the great tragedies, the deaths of husbands or wives or children, the sufferings caused by illness or poverty, or by the children who turn away from their parents or their God or both. These things do happen: God give us strength to cope if and when they come upon us. But quite apart from such obvious and major disasters, there is something about marriage which, when everything has been said about the Sacrament and the splendor, and so rightly, still leaves us with an undercurrent of cynicism. We make little jokes about it. Professor Marra made us laugh earlier by quoting Rosalind's words to Orlando in *As You Like It*, about men being April when they woo, December when they are wed: let me complete the quotation and remind you that Rosalind, an awfully boring girl, by the way, didn't confine it to the men. "Maids are May when they are maids," she goes on, "but the sky changes when they are wives." In much the same vein, Congreve makes one of his characters say that "courtship is to marriage, as a very witty prologue to a very dull play."

The woman who commented so acidly upon that priest's sermon may have had nothing more in mind and memory than the universal fact which these witticisms refer to. Some people see this fact in terms of a war between the sexes. Certainly, the two sexes are so different, so utterly foreign to one another, that such a war — when it does take place — is at least understandable. Somebody once told Chesterton that Americans could get divorced for "incompatibility of temperament!" He was surprised. In that case, he said, it's amazing that any Americans stay married at all: "A man and a woman are incompatible as such." One sees what he meant; and he could say this while glorying in his own marriage.

Let us agree that the sexes are very different, and that the faults of each can be — at times — almost unendurable to the other. To take a small instance: C.S. Lewis says somewhere that in general, fatigue or tiredness makes men want to talk *less* and makes women want to talk *more*. That fact alone must have brought a lot of money to the divorce lawyers. Coleridge hinted at another version of it, very tactfully, when he said: "The most happy marriage that I can picture or imagine to myself would be the union of a deaf man to a blind woman."

The Breakdown of an Institution

Against that background, let me now outline my theme, the particular point I want to make. We all know, we are told incessantly, that marriage as an institution is coming under severe attack nowadays. Many people consider it to be socially obsolete, predicting that it will disappear over the next generation or two, to be replaced by temporary marriages and group marriages and even, for some, by what they call `gay' marriages — an infinitely pathetic word for relationships which quite apart from their immorality tend to be terribly sad.

We also know that there has been a great change in sexual behavior as such. Quite apart from Christian theology and morals, it is the common wisdom and experience of humanity to recognize that sex, while being a good thing in itself, and indeed a holy thing, is also a dangerous thing, an explosive, something that needs to be handled with great caution and restraint. Well, various factors, and the widespread availability of reliable contraceptives is plainly one of them, have now led to a different attitude and to what we now call "the permissive society."

Some people are optimistic about this, seeing here the wise rejection of old hang-ups and neuroses and taboos, and a frank free happy acceptance of what is, after all, one of God's best inventions. But even at a simply social level, I can't share that optimism: this much-celebrated permissive society seems to me to be much more hung-up, much more sexually neurotic than any other society of which I have heard — certainly more than the much-abused Victorian age. The only optimism that I can feel is of a distinctly chilly kind: it seems that the phenomenon isn't likely to last very long, since societies in which family life is weakened and in which sexual permissiveness prevails are thereby weakened in themselves, as societies, and are therefore, in biological or evolutionary or historical terms, unlikely to survive. But there's little comfort in that thought.

At all events, we now face two things: a degree of social breakdown in respect of marriage, and a new and more "permissive" attitude toward sexual behavior inside marriage and outside it as well. And my first suggestion to you, on this occasion, is that we can make a mistake if we exaggerate or oversimplify the relationship between those two things. There plainly is a relationship, a connection. When marriages break down, after all, the trouble often starts with the fact that one party or the other has been sexually attracted to a third party. In less permissive days, Christian morality, fortified by social convention, would very often have caused that illicit passion to be nipped in the bud: adultery would not have taken place, and the marriage would have been kept in being. Nowadays, as we all know, things have a strong tendency to work out differently.

But I think we can make a mistake if we exaggerate the importance of the part played, in such a case, by simple carnal desire and by a consequent simple breach of the moral law. It's more complicated than that. To put it at the crudest possible level: If it's a question of simple carnal desire, the married man or woman is usually well-placed to obtain the satisfaction which the healthy body seeks by nature. And the clergy and other celibates are sometimes baffled by the perversity of a man who, having one woman already, should seek to be burdened with another.

The explanation is, of course, that he wants a change: a physical change, perhaps, but (more importantly) an emotional change. In England, we recently [1973] had a political scandal, rather a mild and modest one, perhaps, as compared to the political scandals of some countries, and it started because a noble lord of ancient family, with a position in the government and a happy marriage, was photographed in what they call "a compromising position" with a prostitute. Interviewed afterwards, he explained with candor that *a man wants a little variety.*

This attitude is not peculiar either to the nobility or to the male sex. The simply carnal element within it is obvious. But what I want to stress is the other element, the emotional element, and the relationship between this and the ideas and expectations that we entertain in connection with love and marriage.

Let me grasp the nettle boldly, and say that the great trouble with present-day marriage is not sexual frustration or over-indulgence or infidelity, but, quite simply, boredom. Boredom is, of course, one of the great troubles of our condition, especially today, and not only in connection with sex and marriage. In all departments of life, we tend to get bored with the over-familiar, and want a change. The Devil exploits this tendency craftily. "The horror of the Same Old Thing" wrote Screwtape, "is one of the most valuable passions we have produced in the human heart — an endless source of heresies in religion, folly in counsel, infidelity in marriage, and inconstancy in friendship." How right he is! And I don't need to tell *this* audience how much Catholic thought of the supposedly enlightened, dynamic, progressive sort is really motivated by that horror of the Same Old Thing — in this case, of the Same Old Church. Boredom is, in fact, the great twentieth-century disease: it is a central theme of that poetic keystone of twentieth-century culture, Eliot's *Waste Land.*

I think it would be honest and realistic to say that the problems of twentieth-century marriage, while working themselves out in so much unchastity, are very substantially rooted in the thing which Screwtape celebrated so proudly — the horror of the Same Old Thing: the Same Old Wife or, of course, Husband.

Now I want to make a few comments upon this very prevailing mood or mentality, insofar as it concerns love and marriage. The trouble, as I see it, is not simply boredom, but boredom turning up where we hadn't expected it. It isn't that people expect too much of marriage and then feel let down: it's that they expect the wrong things. They have in their minds a somewhat unexamined notion of love, and of "being in love" and of the relationship between these things and marriage, which leads them to expect a kind of splendor which is real enough but seldom lasts. When it goes, when boredom sets in, they feel cheated. Hence the disappointment; hence the searching elsewhere, the infidelity, the breakdown.

This is of course a psychological situation, not simply a moral one; and it has its origins in our cultural inheritance, almost in the air we breathe. We who live in the modern Western world often describe it as post-Christian: we know that our civilization has Christian and Catholic origins, and we're often right when we trace even the secular troubles of the day back to the abandonment of those origins and the traditions which stem from them.

And so, in the course of the work that we do as Catholics, we can hope not only to save our souls and spread the Gospel, but also to do something towards the re-establishment of something like a Christian civilization, a Christian commonwealth. Even by the standards of this world, it is needed: it is not only in the standards of this world, it is needed: it is not only in connection with Communism and abortion that the practical alternatives are turning out to be very ugly indeed.

But we need to remember that within the Western tradition, we inherit (and from the Middle Ages, the "Ages of Faith" as we call them too simply) various habits of the mind that are not Catholic or Christian at all. Because these habits of the mind are familiar, we can overlook them; because they are old, not stemming recently from the modern world's apostasy, we can easily overlook the danger that they represent.

Where Charity And Love Should Prevail

The thing which I have in mind can be called "the romantic theory of love." We all know that "love" lies at the heart of our religion and is in fact its only commandment; we also know (I hope) that "love" is a very complicated idea, and that the charity or *agape* of which St. Paul speaks is not at all the same thing as the predatory and insincere sort of people-eating which the sexual liberators disguise under that sacred name of love.

What we sometimes forget (I suggest) is that the word "love" can refer also to something a good deal loftier than that, chaster than that too, ancient, and most traditional, but still most un-Christian and very dangerous.

In developing this subject, I shall be drawing on a book which I'm sure many of you have read: *Passion and Society,* by Denis de Rougemont. It's a very good book: I've been told that it's a bit shaky historically, but psychologically and theologically it's right on the ball. Its author, de Rougemont, distinguishes love — in the sense of charity or *agape* — from what he calls "passion": his great thesis is that society and civilization and marriage and happiness all depend upon charity, but are undermined and attacked by "passion."

What does he mean by "passion"? Oversimplifying somewhat, you can say that love becomes "passion," in this special sense of the word, insofar as it is valued directly, for its own sake, as a state of mind. We've all had some experience of it. In adolescence, weren't there times when we were in love with the idea of being in love? And wasn't that an entirely self-regarding state of mind, a form of self-love? And perhaps we then, and while in that state, seized upon some person of the opposite sex and forcibly cast him or her for the role of a loved one? And if so, wasn't the *reality* of that person's existence an object almost of indifference to us? We saw her (or him) through a kind of golden haze, and we enjoyed it immensely.

Now if we married in quite that state, we came down to earth with rather a bump: we found out that it was an actual human being that we'd become fastened to, not a goddess or a mythological hero. Marriage (in other words) kills passion: passion in de Rougemont's sense (some would call it *Eros*) *is* the enemy of marriage in return. A man under the influence of passion or Eros doesn't want an actual woman: he wants a *princesse lointaine,* a dream-goddess, a vision of total and perfect femininity. He is therefore likely to hop from girl to girl, conquering them one after another, but finding disappointment in each. Reality — human reality included, sexual reality included — is always a let-down for him. He may come positively to prefer fantasy.

There's a story of some soldiers who were going on leave and planned to go to a house of ill repute. But one man didn't want to go there: he said he was going to stay behind in the barracks and indulge his erotic fantasies. Why? "Well," he said, "you meet a better class of girl that way."

His state of mind is a common one. There's a vast appetite for fantasy-sex nowadays: the indulging of it has become big business: even this very hotel includes a moderately discreet section of that market place. I take this to be very bad. It's bad enough when young people fornicate or even older people: I take it to be worse still when people turn away from actual sex – which is, after all, real, was made by God, and always includes some element or possibility of *agape* – towards, say *Playboy* magazine.

The point I want to make, at this stage, is that great sexual evil is not necessarily, or most destructively, a matter of actual illicit copulation. Passion (in de Rougemont's sense) is in fact a pull *away from* actual consummation, which spoils the dream and raises the possibility of all kinds of humdrum things like babies and domesticity. In de Rougemont's book, the influence of passion upon Western notions of love is chiefly worked out in terms of the myth of Tristan and Isolde; and the whole point and ecstasy of their passion lay in its non-fulfillment. "When Tristan carries off Isolde to the forest, where there is nothing any longer to obstruct their union, the demon of passion sets down a drawn sword between their two bodies." Passion is essentially a seeking of the impossible, the unattainable: it is a flight from reality: ultimately, it is a seeking of death.

Two years age, I addressed this Forum on the subject of Gnostic and Manichaean trends in modern culture and especially in modern religion, as some of you will remember if you were present and if you were awake at the time. In a sense, what I'm now saying follows on from that. As de Rougemont shows, the cult of passion or romantic love or Eros is of medieval but not of Catholic origin: it stems from the Manichaean movements of the Middle Ages, the Albigensian and Catharist heresies, and the associated cult of the troubadours and of what they called "courtly love." We may be living, for the most part, in a post-Christian culture but where love and marriage are concerned, our attitudes and especially our expectations are still strongly colored by the fact that we live in a post-Albigensian, post-Catharist culture, and one that is now swinging back in that direction.

Being In Love Isn't Enough

I wonder if you'll agree with what I'm getting at. We over-romanticize, overvalue, overload the experience of being *in* love; we expect it to carry burdens that only *agape* or real charity can carry. Thus comes the boredom, the disappointment, the breakdown. It is in the very air we breathe. Consider, for example, the convention which makes a marriage the *ending* of a romantic novel or movie: consider our sentimentality about a wedding. The Church has always been more realistic about human nature, more cynical, if you like. I quote from Msgr. Ronald Knox:

> "She [the Church] says: 'Oh, you want to get married, do you? That means, you want to imitate the action of Jesus Christ in the Incarnation. Well, God bless you; you will want all the grace I can rout out for you if you are going to do that, a whole trousseau of grace!' She thinks at once not of the fun you are going to have, but of the qualities you will need."

You and I agree, of course, in principle; but isn't there a little undertow in our minds, suggesting that the Church is here being a bit too pessimistic? After all, these two young people are *in love* and utterly dedicated to each other: their eyes shine, it's a joy to behold them.

We all feel grief and regret when confronted by mere promiscuity, and by the emotional and psychological chaos it causes. But don't we all feel that we're on fairly safe and happy ground when a marriage is soundly based upon the mutual experience that we call "being in love"?

Most of us know that experience: it's a bit like Heaven and a bit like lunacy. It's a marvelous thing, one of God's great gifts to humanity. But it isn't enough. It can launch a marriage but can very seldom keep it in being: before long, the burden will need to be taken over by affection, by friendship, by a sense of duty, and by *agape* or charity.

But these are humdrum virtues, and "passion" detests the humdrum, seeking always the ecstasy of new and preferably unsatisfied desire. Hell, with its clever strategy, thus contrives to make marriage extremely difficult for those under the influence of the romantic idea of love, of "passion." "We have done this" says Screwtape, "through the poets and the novelists by persuading the humans that a curious, and usually short-lived, experience which they call 'being in love' is the only respectable ground for marriage; that marriage can, and ought to, render this excitement permanent; and that a marriage which does not do so is no longer binding." The consequences of Hell's strategy, in this field, are all about us. Our modern marriages get into trouble, not only and perhaps not chiefly because of direct sexual temptation, but also because of heretical elements in our society's concept of love.

If I concluded here, you might think I was against this business of being in love. I'm not: I thing it's terrific, a great and holy thing if we don't overload it. It can, in fact, open our eyes to the God's-eye view of things. Coventry Patmore, an English Catholic poet of the nineteenth century, put it well:

> *Love wakes men, once a lifetime each;*
> *They lift their heavy lids, and look;*
> *And, lo, what one sweet page can teach,*
> *They read with joy, then shut the book.*
> *And some give thanks, and some blaspheme,*
> *And most forget; but, either way,*
> *That and the child's unheeded dream*
> *Is all the light of all their day.*
> > –Patmore, "The Revelation"

Well, to get the holy vision just once, from love, is much better than not getting it at all! We've all seen it happen: we've all met some pleasant and virtuous young man who's suddenly fallen head-over-heels in love and tells us about his girl. She's quite unique: nobody was ever so beautiful, so intelligent, so witty, so kind, so marvelous in every way. Then we meet her; and he comes up afterwards to see whether we share his estimate of her. "Nay, but you who do not love her, Is she not pure gold, my mistress?" It can be an embarrassing question! We met her, and we thought she was a very nice girl, but very ordinary, not very different from a million others. And so we smile inwardly at the young man's infatuation: "And therefore is wing'd Cupid painted blind" we think.

But he's right and we're wrong. Under influences which are

chiefly glandular, he has come to see one of God's creatures in something like the light in which God sees all of His creatures *all* the time. And the way God sees things, that's how they really are: "The world is charged with the grandeur of God," as Hopkins says, and it's only our blindness that prevents us from seeing the fact and so enables us to be bored in this wonderful and delicate creation and in that blazing and sacramental thing, that embodiment of Christ's relationship with His Church, a marriage.

God sees His creation through a lover's eyes. If only we could learn from the experience of being in love and do the same! If we did, we would never talk about ordinary, dull, suburban, bourgeois, boring people again: we would see them, rather through Traherne's eyes:

> The Men! O what venerable and reverend creatures did the aged seem! Immortal cherubims! And young men glittering and sparkling Angels, and maids strange seraphic pieces of life and beauty! Boys and girls tumbling in the street, and playing, were moving jewels. I knew not that they were born or should die; but all things abided eternally as they were in their proper places.
>
> –Traherne, *Centuries of Meditations*

This I take to be a fully Christian view of what people are. Against it, we have the Gnostic, Manichaean, or existentialist view, according to which the visible universe, people included, is meaningless and absurd at the best, horrifyingly evil at the worst.

There is thus a sense, far transcending mere morality, in which our marriages need to be Christian. May God grant us to see our wives and husbands, and then all creation, and eventually God Himself, in the light of that sudden and blinding illumination which knocked us endways at the moment when we first fell in love.

Christopher Derrick spoke at the Ninth National Wanderer Forum. Derrick was an administrator at the University of London and served as a literary consultant to one of London's most distinguished publishing houses. He authored several book reviews for both English and American publications and several books on the moral and social teaching of the Catholic Church, including *Trimming the Ark*, and *The Delicate Creation: Towards a Theology of the Environment*.

POISONED PASTURES

Dr. Charles E. Rice
Notre Dame University

Note: This talk was given shortly after the 1973 U.S. Supreme Court decision allowing abortion, when public anger over this outrage against life was at its highest point. While it may seem outdated to review this, there is a need to know what went before in order to understand what to do in the future.

The first thing to do, is to dispel the notion of somber defeatism that is felt in some of what we call the orthodox Catholic movement or the right-to-life movement. I have to confess that I'm an optimist, but I think it might be worthwhile to put the problem in some kind of focus.

Within the past week or ten days, there were two stories in the paper: in New Jersey, a young man went into the hospital where his brother was lying incurably paralyzed as the result of a motorcycle accident, and he went in and shot him in the head — killed him, put him out of his misery. And a few days later, on Long Island, there was a proceeding started by the district attorney against a doctor who administered a fatal injection to a terminally ill cancer patient who had only two days to live.

And I wonder why there's so much coming out at this time on this particular topic of euthanasia. Euthanasia does not refer to Chinese children, it refers to a Greek word that simply means "happy death" and it refers to the practice of putting people out of their misery, that is, active euthanasia. Illegal euthanasia would also consist of withholding ordinary means of treatment. The law here pretty well corresponds to the teaching of the Church, particularly as articulated by Pius XII in this area.

But when you look at news stories like this, you realize that there's something afoot here, and in the most recent issue of *The Humanist* magazine, there was an article by Paul Blanshard who was resurrected for the purpose, and Edd Doerr in which they said that the abortion decisions [*Roe v Wade, Doe v Bolton*] were the most severe defeat for the Roman

Catholic hierarchy in the history of American law and they said, "We feel like a champagne dinner." Here are their exact words:

> "We feel like a champagne dinner in honor of the U.S. Supreme Court for its January decision on abortion....The Blackmun decisions, in which the only Catholic on the Court (Brennan) concurred, constitute the most direct defeat for the Catholic Hierarchy in the history of American law."
>
> –Blanshard and Doerr, "A Glorious Victory,"
> *The Humanist*, May-June, 1973, p.5)

Well, I don't think it looks like a champagne dinner, but I can understand why they would feel like a champagne dinner, because the decisions were a tremendous victory. We can understand what is going on and what we have to do about it only if we put it in some kind of focus. And the focus is that what has happened in this country is that a new religion has been established as the State religion of the United States. That religion, of course, is secular humanism — secularism. Make no mistake about it, it *is* a religion. And it has been established by the Supreme Court. Really you can't blame the Court for this, and I blame them for a lot of things, because it really reflected a national consensus of indifference in this matter.

The Law of God vs. The Law of the State

Let me mention this, the process that occurs is that the State tends to liberate itself from any standard which is higher than its own law. There's no standard of right and wrong higher than the State, so the State becomes the standard of morality and morality ultimately is determined not by the natural law, the Law of God, but rather by majority vote in Congress or in Supreme Court. It was interesting that the most recent Harris poll [April, 1973] pointed out that prior to the abortion rulings of January 22, 1973, only 42% of the American people favored abortion on request. Since those rulings six months ago, the figure has gone up to 56%. And Harris commented that it's a fairly common occurrence that when the Court articulates something, then popular opinion swings into line (*American Medical News*, April 30, 1973). But you see what's happening is that the government itself is becoming the arbiter of morality. These are people who believe that abortion on request is moral. Why do they believe this? Because the Supreme Court says so. Now how did we get to this position? Let me digress if I may, and go into just a little bit of the constitutional aspects of this.

Our First Amendment contains two religion clauses. One, Congress shall make no law respecting an establishment of religion. This was designed to ensure neutrality on the part of government as against religions. The other clause says, nor prohibiting the free exercise thereof. This was intended to protect the free exercise of religion by all people, atheists, agnostics, even Catholics. But what was the interpretation of that first clause? That clause which was designed to make government neutral as to religion, the interpretation of it quite clearly, inescapably, was that religion was defined as including a belief in God. The idea was that you couldn't have a religion without God, anymore than you could have baseball without a ball.

Justice Story, who himself was a Unitarian, put this very clearly:

> "Probably at the time of the adoption of the Constitution, and of the First Amendment to it...the general if not the universal sentiment in America was, that Christianity ought to receive encouragement from the State so far as was not incompatible with the private rights of conscience and the freedom of religious worship. An attempt to level all religions, and to make it a matter of State policy to hold all in utter indifference, would have created universal disapprobation, if not universal indignation.

> "...The real object of the Amendment was not to countenance, much less to advance, Mahometanism, or Judaism, or infidelity, by prostrating Christianity; but to exclude all rivalry among Christian sects, and to prevent any national ecclesiastical establishment which should give to a hierarchy the exclusive patronage of the national government"

> –Story, *Commentaries on the Constitution of the United States — 1874 and 1877* (1891)

Justice Story elaborated on this. He said the purpose of this Amendment was not to prevent government from encouraging religion. It was not to prostrate Christianity. He said the general feeling at the time was that Christianity should be encouraged. And this was true. I could give you a lot of quotations and citations to reinforce that. But the idea was clear, that government in the United States — and this applies to State and Federal governments now — was supposed to encourage theism, at least; perhaps actually Christianity.

But let's just talk about theism. Government was supposed to encourage theism and maintain neutrality as among theistic sects, that is, maintain neutrality as among all religions because if you weren't theistic you weren't a religion; your free exercise of religion was protected in that sense, but you weren't a religion in terms of the government's duty to maintain neutrality.

Changing Definitions

What happened? In 1961, the Supreme Court began to change all this and they did it in a very innocuous seeming way. I like to play around with this a little bit by saying that Roy Torcaso really brought about the abortion decisions. Now I don't think you really know who Roy Torcaso is. He had his name attached to a Supreme Court case. He's a man in Maryland who applied for a job as a notary public and he was denied the job because the Maryland constitution required him to declare his belief in God. The Supreme Court ruled that this was unconstitutional because it prefers religions that believe in God over religions that don't believe in God. And then they said that government must maintain neutrality among such religions. They said the power and prestige of the State of Maryland is placed on the side of those religions that believe in God and then, in a footnote to Justice Black's opinion, they said: "Among religions in this Country which do not teach what would commonly be considered a belief in the existence of God are Buddhism, Taoism, ethical culture, secular humanism and others."

Now this really could be defended as a free exercise case. You shouldn't keep a guy out of a routine State job because he's an atheist. But the point was that two years later, in the Supreme Court school-prayer decisions, the Court adopted this new definition of religion with respect to the other part of the First Amendment so that the Court now decreed that the Government must be neutral as among religions. Well that was the basic rule anyway, but now, religions include non-theistic religions. So the mandate is that government must be neutral not among theistic religions, while professing a belief in God and encouraging religion generally, but rather must try to be neutral as between the two great classes of religions, the theistic and the nontheistic. You don't have to be very bright to realize that that isn't possible.

Justice Brennan, in his concurring opinion in the 1963 school-prayer case, talked about this and he hit it right on the head. He was trying to reassure people. He said, don't worry, people, we will not have to bite the words, "In God we trust," from out of our coins. He said the words "Under God" in the Pledge of Allegiance are not necessarily invalid. Why? And this is what he said, "Because they may merely recognize the historical fact that our Nation *was believed to have been founded under God*" (*Abingdon School District v Schenpp,* 374 U.S. 203,304 -1963 emphasis added).

It's quite clear. If a public official were to stand up and say, "One Nation under God," and intend it to be an affirmation of fact that God exists, just as this lectern exists, that is unconstitutional. Because under the new routine, the new Supreme Court dispensation, the Government must be neutral as between theism and nontheism which includes both atheism and agnosticism.

So the little kid in the school goes up and asks his teacher, "Hey, is the Declaration of Independence true when it says in four places that there's a God?" And what does the teacher say? If the teacher says, "Yes, it's true," that's unconstitutional, because it affirms the truth of theism. If the teacher says, "It's untrue," that's unconstitutional, because that is a governmental preference of atheism. So the teacher says, "Go home, run home, ask your mother."

The teacher now, speaking as the agent of the State, has to say, "I cannot answer that because on behalf of the State I cannot state as a fact whether or not God exists." In other words, the existence of God is unknown or unknowable to the Government. And this is a drastic shift from what went before and it is the classical definition of agnosticism — it is secular humanism.

Cardinal O'Boyle pointed this out well in 1971, when he talked about the public schools. He said: Let's not kid ourselves, they are teaching a new religion, secular humanism. They call it pragmatism but it is secular humanism because God is excluded:

> "Of course, it may be argued that the public schools need not favor any particular religion or religion at all, for they can proceed on strictly humanistic, pragmatic and secular conceptions. But this is precisely the point. To proceed in this way is itself to establish a religion — secular humanism — and to favor this religion over all others"
>
> *–Catholic Currents,* Nov. 15th, 1971, p. 3

Now where does that lead us? What happens now? We're talking about abortion. Suddenly I've gone on rambling about notaries public. Well, there is a connection. I can't prove this, but I'm convinced that once the State liberates itself from the conviction that there is a standard of right and wrong higher than the State, then there is no protection against tyranny. Thomas Jefferson said it well, "Can the liberties of a Nation be secure when we have removed a conviction that those liberties are the gift of God?" And he said no. And we have now, over the past dozen years, the spectacle of the government of the United States affirmatively committed to the proposition that we don't know whether God exists or not, in effect, affirmatively committed to a new State religion which is secular humanism.

And you can see the consequences. You can see it in government promotion of birth control, you can see it in government usurpation of authority over children in the schools by invading areas of parental concern, you can see it in other areas as well. You can see it pre-eminently in abortion.

Target: The Family

Now what is the framework in which we are going to put this? Well, oddly enough, in 1961, the same year that Roy Torcaso was fighting for his notary public job, there was a book published in England and it was a series of essays by leading humanists, *The Humanist Frame*. The whole pitch was for what we see around us today. It could very well have been written in 1973, or better yet, 1984, because it is a blueprint above all, for the removal of the supernatural from society; for as Sir Julian Huxley said in the lead article about the removal of absolutes: *there can be no absolutes*. Of course that is itself an absolute. But what he means by that is we don't want any of that theistic nonsense. And contraception was seen as a great social boon, a great benefit. There are a lot of other comments in there that are quite appropriate, but the one that is interesting to me is the comment by Barbara Wootton and she said, the victory of the humanist ideas is really the product of the failure – of the decline rather — of organized religion, particularly Christianity. And that's true, because the victory has been accomplished and is being accomplished by the other side — temporarily, because we're going to win — the victory is being temporarily accomplished by the other side only because we have not really joined the fight.

Let's take the prime area here. That's the family. We're talking about *Casti Connubii,* a great encyclical. But let's not kid ourselves. The prime target of this whole humanist drive, the prime target of the humanist State — the secular humanist State — is the family. We have had, for example, a tremendous increase in divorces. In 1960, 25.8% of marriages ended in annulment or divorce. In 1971, 35%. Now what does that mean in figures? It means that in 1971 there were 2,196,000 weddings in this Country. In the very same year, there were 768,000 marriages dissolved by divorce or annulment (*U.S. News and World Report,* Aug. 14, 1972, p.130). That's a bad thing.

You know what the drive is against the family in other areas, the sex-education madness, not only in public but also in parochial schools; the whole business of coercing people to engage in family planning — I don't mean that in a good sense, I mean contraception; the whole idea of usurping the parental control over children by undue and unwise testing and evaluations and social engineering in the schools; the legalization of homosexual acts — what has that to do with the family? It has a lot to do with it, because when you legalize homosexual acts, you legalize not *de jure*, not in terms of the law, but you legalize *in fact* homosexual marriages. So what? All I'm saying is that if it doesn't make any difference to a society whether boys marry girls or other boys, that society has gone beyond the line of clinical insanity. I think that you just have to put it in that context. But that sort of thing is exactly the necessary, the inevitable result of the establishment of secularism as the State religion in this Country.

Pius XI put his finger on it. He said that the root evil — he used that term — the root evil is the idea that the family and marriage, marriage particularly, is instituted by man, not by God. Well sure, if marriage is instituted by man you can play around with it, you can change it, you can use alternative things, you can use all kinds of happy little experiments, the same way you can experiment with traffic regulations. Now here you have really many examples and it gets kind of bizarre.

You know, the ecology business is good in a sense, in a way. I don't mean to knock it in its legitimate manifestations, but I really scratch my head when I see things, for example, in one case involving the Sierra Club, a year ago, William Zero Douglas, Justice of the Supreme Court, wrote an opinion in which he said, now catch this: Inanimate objects, such as rivers and trees should have rights. I kid you not, people, that's what he said, inanimate objects should have rights so that people could sue to protect the rights of those inanimate objects: "Inanimate objects, such as rivers and trees have rights so that those rights could be asserted to block the commercial development of remote areas" (*Sierra Club v Morton,* 405 U.S. 727, 741 - 1972). Now guess where he was in the abortion case. Because there's this little baby that's kicking around in the mother's womb doesn't mean it has to have any rights that have to be protected. This gets to be idiotic.

Now there are a few very basic things I want to mention. One thing is that I think we have been entirely too defensive on the basic issue of contraception. We tend to skulk around corners and mumble in our beards as if *Humanae Vitae* were a skin disease. It isn't, it is a great encyclical. What is insufficiently noticed is the connection between contraception and abortion.

Contraception has its own evil aspects; venereal disease is one of them. You know, in 1971, 25.8% of all the gonorrhea cases were had by kids under the age of twenty. In 1971, in the fifteen-to-nineteen-year age group, out of every 100,000 kids, 808 had a venereal disease. You know what the figure was five years earlier? 436.1 (*New York Times,* April 18th, 1973, p.7, col.1). And those who are in the field say quite frankly that it's because of easy contraception.

And Abortion Follows

But let's look at something else here. Let's look at the connection between that and abortion. You know some of the pro-life people and the opponents of abortion are so afraid of the contraception issue, that I think they do a disservice to the whole movement. Kenneth Whitehead in his book, *Respectable Killing: The New Abortion Imperative,* quoted a statement to this effect by Prof. Ralph Potter, a Protestant, and he said, in effect that when children become considered, not the gift of God but rather something attributable to rotten luck or bad timing, the stage is set for abortion. And it's true. Here are his exact words:

> "When a new habit of mind now attributes new life to 'rotten luck' in the practice of contraception rather than to the purposeful will of a merciful God, neglect of the counter-measure of abortion becomes irrational and superstitious retreat from the possibility of exercising control of one's destiny. Denial of accessibility to abortion comes to be seen by many as a violation of civil liberty."

Abortion is the most widely used method of birth control. Did you know that? A few years ago, the United Nations estimated there were over 30,000,000 abortions a year throughout the world. Now the figure is much higher. But consider the connection between the two. You cannot have a contraceptive society, you cannot have a secular humanist society, and not have abortion. That is true because your objections to abortion, if you're talking about the pragmatic approach, become functional — that is it doesn't work; or aesthetic — that is, it is distasteful.

Part of our problem is that over the past generation, not only has the State established secular humanism as the national religion, but we have had the ascendency in jurisprudential circles of the utilitarian, pragmatic approach. We no longer talk about the natural law of things. And in the law schools, the dominant jurisprudence has been utilitarian and essentially pragmatic. But under the natural law, there is disagreement as to what it forbids. And it doesn't make any sense to try to articulate it without bringing in the fact that there is one arbiter of natural law and that's the Holy Father, the Pope.

I would suggest that the reason why the American experiment has degenerated is because it started off with good intentions, particularly the intention to encourage Christianity and theism in general. It started off with a generalized respect for the natural law, but it failed to acknowledge the moral arbiter who is essential and that is the Vicar of Christ. You had a situation in the American State, in which the moral authority of the Vicar of Christ was not recognized, and then the governing approach, to determining what is right and/or wrong in the law became one of consensus, the greatest good of the greatest number. As determined by whom? As determined by majority or as determined by the Supreme Court. Well, if that's the standard or if law is designed only to adjust competing interests, then there really is no enduring objection to abortion or to anything else.

On the contrary, law is designed, as Thomas Aquinas pointed out, for the common good and to promote virtue, and law must be in harmony, not only with the natural moral law but also with the Divine law which means the Ten Commandments — and that includes "Thou shalt not kill." And we've got to get back to that. We cannot believe that we can cure a broken leg with a Band-aid anymore than we can believe that we can redress everything wrong with American society just by adopting an abortion amendment. That is essential, but we have got to do more: we have to bring about a total spiritual regeneration in this Country so that people recognize from the vantage point of their needs that, in fact, we are under God, not just as a sentimental observance, but simply as a matter of fact. We've got to do that.

We Need An Amendment

Now how about a tactic? How about, for example, the abortion problem? Unfortunately, we really need a constitutional amendment to deal with the abortion question. There are three essential requirements of an amendment for it to be acceptable and don't take anything less. The amendment must be prohibitory. You're going to get the great cop-out argument, that we should turn these things back to the States. Let the States legalize or not abortion as they choose. That would be like fighting World War II for the professed aim of giving each location in Germany the option to decide whether or not to have an extermination camp. And it would make just as much sense. In fact, the amendment has been introduced, the Whitehurst amendment [1973], and you're going to find a lot of people, Catholic people, maybe even Catholic bishops, who want to get rid of a hot potato, who will support this thing, throw it back to the States. But you know, the Whitehurst amendment, the States' rights amendment that would give the States the right to legalize abortion or to prohibit it as they choose would not even stop abortions in the States that want to stop them. This is because it would leave undisturbed the basic fallacy of the Supreme Court decisions, which is that the child in the womb is a nonperson. And therefore, he would become a nonperson under State constitutional provisions because State courts would follow the Supreme Court, because the Whitehurst amendment does not overrule the Supreme Court on the basic proposition. It is a dangerous thing.

The Buckley amendment is well-intended, but it is unduly vague. And give the man credit, he stood up, he did a job, and he's trying — he is sincerely opposed to abortion. But it's got to be very precise. Now the Buckley amendment is a prohibitory amendment. So is the Hogan amendment — the Hogan-Helms amendment or the Helms-Hogan amendment, depending on whether you like it alphabetical or chronological.

The first requirement is that the amendment must be prohibitory. That is, that it must prohibit abortions instead of leaving it up to the States. The second requirement is that the abortion amendment must apply right from the beginning of life which is the moment of fertilization. The moment of conception as it is in the Hogan amendment, I believe, is adequate to do the job, but if somebody comes up with a better phrasing on it, fine, that's great; but let us not yield for one single moment on that basic issue that it has to apply from the beginning of life. And the third proposition I would suggest is that the amendment must make sure that there will be no legalization of euthanasia.

I think those things can be done. And we have the Hogan amendment, introduced now by Sen. Helms of North Carolina, who is, of course, following the orders of the Pope as a good Baptist would. And I think it is beginning to gel. You have a general consensus among right-to-life people throughout the country on these three basic points, a mandatory amendment from fertilization that should cover euthanasia. And we're going to go with it.

Now how do we go with it? We go with it by coercing, if necessary, legislators, congressmen to support it. We go after them and we tell them, "If you won't support us, if you're not with us on these points, we'll beat your political brains out" — figuratively. This can be done, it's been done in other parts of the country. It was done in New York, where the New York legislature passed abortion on request in 1970 and as a result of strong-arm tactics directed against legislators, they reversed themselves in 1972. What were those strong-arm tactics? They were, "Harry, if you go the wrong way on this, you're going to have to look for a job." And it worked. And the legislature repealed the permissive abortion law. Governor Rockefeller, of course, vetoed the repeal. Incidentally, he vetoed it in the same week that he proclaimed "Healthy Baby Week."

The abortion amendment question can be isolated. We can go for an abortion amendment and say nothing about contraception. We can do that and it is not necessary that people who support us on the abortion issue also buy the whole package on contraception. I would not condition the success of an abortion amendment on that issue. Let's keep those things separate as legislation, because the amendment itself would have nothing to do with contraception.

But let's make this perfectly clear. We cannot fulfill our responsibility if we ignore the contraception issue. I think quite frankly it's about time that we had some voice although I hate organizations. I think it's about time that we had a new voice, maybe a new organization that would come out and say two things: it would come out and would say, first of all, we are opposed to all abortions, period, paragraph, whether you say it's for the life of the mother, or the life of anybody. We're opposed to them and we insist they be outlawed by the strongest possible language. Secondly, we are opposed to all governmental involvement in family planning.

I take a position personally, that ultimately, government should restrict the sale and distribution of contraceptives because they are a social evil as well as a moral evil. I don't say that they should prohibit their use, because you can't prohibit their use without invading privacy — how do you get your evidence? But I do say that although I strongly espouse restrictions on contraceptives, I am not, emphatically not, going to tie that to the abortion amendment so as to make that also an element of the abortion amendment.

However, the government has no business in this area, and the evil here is that the secular humanist State, liberated from any concern for a higher law — because it doesn't exist as far as they're concerned — is using every weapon in the book to manipulate and control people and contraception is one of them as well as abortion and sterilization. Let's get the government out of that area and let's not be ashamed to say it.

The third thing that such an organization should do would be very simple. It would be to encourage the reading of *Humanae Vitae*. Now what could be difficult about that? Consider what the situation would be in this country if everybody read *Humanae Vitae*. I mean, if you look at the public schools, I don't think everybody *could* read *Humanae Vitae,* but everybody who could handle it read *Humanae Vitae*. But suppose everybody read *Humanae Vitae*. Or suppose every Catholic read *Humanae Vitae*. How many loudmouths and windbags have you seen who have pontificated against it without having any idea what's in it? If you want to go further, how much better things would be if one Catholic out of ten read *Humanae Vitae* or one Catholic out of a hundred? Why can't we do that, why can't we come out affirmatively and say we're not ashamed to take the Church's position here. We're not ashamed, we're going to come out here and say that contraception, abortion, sterilization are all bad.

We Must Stand Firm For Life

We demand a constitutional amendment on abortion, period. If necessary, we would accept an amendment that would not forbid abortion to save the life of the mother provided it left the door open to eventual repeal of those laws, but we want our objective and that is to stop all killing, all deliberate killing of babies. Secondly, our objective is to remove government entirely from this area. And thirdly, our objective is not just to change the laws, because we're not going to get anywhere by tinkering with laws. Our objective is really to revolutionize American society in a spiritual way by recalling people to the realities of God, Christianity, and of the Church.

Archbishop John Murphy of Cardiff, Wales [1905-1995] made a comment once and he said:

> "It is the Church which fights for the unborn child, for the rights of parents to educate their children, for the dignity of the marriage contract, for the dignity of the individual being. And in some secular humanistic future, when the only sin will be pain, the only evil ill health; when childbearing will be looked upon as a disease, and terminal illnesses will not be tolerated, when it is just possible that the free, human beings will be forbidden to have a child, or a smoke, or a drink, save by prescription of the National Health; in that cold, clinical future, you will search in vain for the rebels, save in the ranks of the Catholic Church."

The problem with that is that the cold clinical future he talked about is our present pretty much, and we've got to get out and do some things. We've got to get out and we've got to fight. We've got to adhere to principle, we've got to stand up and say we're loyal to the Pope, the Vicar of Christ. We've got to do more than just accommodate with secular humanism, we've got to rechristianize American society and ultimately, to disestablish the State religion of secularism. And we're going to do that through the power of prayer. We're also going to do it through hard work, but primarily through the power of prayer, because this whole tendency is foreign to nature and to God.

And we've got to stand firm. We must never compromise on any of these points. As the Declaration of Independence said, there is a law of nature and of nature's God and this whole modern anti-life society is so foreign to that law of nature and nature's God that the only way to correct it is through reliance on what the Declaration of Independence called Divine Providence and with the help of God — not just with the help of God, but solely by His help and generosity. He is going to do it and we are going to help Him. We are going to be His instruments.

Dr. Charles E. Rice delivered this address at the Ninth National Wanderer Forum. Rice taught law at Fordham University, Notre Dame School of Law, and was associated with the founding of Ave Maria School of Law. He has served on the governing board of Franciscan University and EWTN, and on the Educational Appeal Board of the Department of Education. He is editor of the *American Journal of Jurisprudence* and has authored several books on issues in the right to life movement, politics, and law, and has made several television appearances on EWTN. He is chairman of the Wanderer Forum Foundation.

SAME SEX MARRIAGE: WHEN TWO CAN NEVER BE ONE

Frank Morriss
Wheat Ridge, Colorado

The term oxymoron is derived from a Greek phrase meaning "pointedly foolish." And that is exactly what the talk about same-sex "marriage" amounts to, for it contains within itself a contradiction as great, say, as the idea would be for motionless football or batless baseball. Were some paralyzed individual to demand the "right" to play football, the American Civil Liberties Union might support him on the grounds of non-discrimination. But the nature of football is a game in which players must run, pass the ball, kick it, advance it over the goal line – all of these making the demands listed above for inclusion beyond reason. And if some batter allergic to wood would claim the "right" to use something stained or painted to appear to be wood, that too would be oxymoronic, since in its conception by its inventor, baseball demands a wooden bat.

There are essentials to all realities, whether creations of God, as is marriage, or arrangements of humans such as the interrelationships making up society. It is essential for realities that they not be reduced to superficialities or mere practicalities. That would loosen our grip on reality itself. Honoring lust rather than the act of love put to God's service is inevitable in the recognition of "same-sex marriage," since that concept's purpose is to protect the dignity of those abusing their sexual faculties by deliberate surrender to passion. Sexual pleasure in the marital act of love, on the other hand, is God's gift rewarding and encouraging the use of sexuality to further His purposes, not man's.

When we intrude our own will in the matter, we are challenging Him, in effect, to use miracles to continue the human race as we arrogate sexuality to our own use, preferring to have the passion but destroy or prevent its consequence. That consequence is new life, the possibility of which ennobles sex, whereas lust defiles it.

A person who might use a beautiful diamond to do evil – let us say to lure a weak person into some sort of violence – would be guilty of defiling the gem's beauty, and the tribute that beauty stirs in appreciation of its creation. So, too, does lust work to the defilement of the beauty of sex when it (sex) is not used in conformity to the full nature of man, which includes rationality and the obedience to God rationality enjoins. Lust, which contraceptive sex, sodomistic sex, impure hedonistic sex serve, works the same sort of defilement of the beauty of the intimacy of man and woman that God made possible by sexual difference. Lust calls for privacy in order for those given to it to escape shame. Sex within the sanctity of marriage calls for the sort of privacy we give to our highest moments of worship.

We do not cast pearls before swine, nor should we insult sex by robbing it of purpose. Husband and wife in their sexual intimacy are practicing a sort of piety – the piety of married men and women obeying God in sexual union compatible with His creative desire. Scripture refers to it as becoming "one flesh." And that term can in one meaning be taken as referring to the result of sexual intercourse both immediately in husband and wife becoming one by the marital act, but also as a result of the act in the ongoing unity achieved by male and female procreative elements combining as a new, unique human person – the conceived child.

None of this can be achieved genuinely and naturally by those of the same sex. Homosexual acts are simulations of sexual intercourse, for these acts cannot involve the complementarity of male/female sexual union. And these simulated acts are thus infertile, with true union of the generative elements rendered impossible by such activities within the same gender. Some simulation of married life may be possible, including enlarging cohabitation to include other men's and women's children; but if cohabitation alone supplied the essence of marriage, mankind long ago would have called that sociological condition a marriage. Instead, mankind universally has seen as essential to marriage the willingness and capacity of man and woman to give themselves fully, completely, and in the ideal, exclusively, to one another, that giving being fulfilled in the profound intimacy of sexual union. Today's society should ask itself if it wishes to demean that understanding of marriage by giving equal recognition to those demanding it, but who cannot achieve this complete union by their own natures and the nature of their "arrangements."

The very word "marriage" argues against doing so. Its root etymologically is the word for man, i.e., male, and therefore by connotation one caring for property. The word for woman can include her capacity to be a wife, that is "womb-man" to a husband. In keeping with this, the 17th century clergyman, Samuel Purchas, describes woman as "a house builded for generation and gestation, whence our [English] language calls her woman, womb-man." John A. Ryan, writing on the history of marriage for the original *Catholic Encyclopedia*, explains, "…the phrase 'husband and wife' implies mutual rights of sexual intercourse."

So vital is such a right in its exercise, the Supreme Pontiff may dissolve a valid marriage that is not consummated by that intercourse, whereas the contract validly made and consummated is dissolved only by death, and no human has authority to do so. Fr. Augustus Lemhkulh, S.J., writing in the same work on the *Moral and Canonical Aspects of Marriage*, seems to attribute the authority of the Church to dissolve marriages *ratum non consummatum* (valid but not consummated) to the interpretation that this does not contradict the pronunciation, "What God hath joined, let no man put asunder…." This suggests that the joining intended for husband and wife in the state of marriage is by virtue of the marital act, the proper and complementary union of their sexual organs.

In this view, which is certainly the accepted one of Catholic understanding and doctrine, it follows that two or more men *cannot* marry nor can two or more women. They are physiologically incapable of fulfilling part of the marriage contract that is of its essence. Whatever equality of rights may be considered by civil authority as demanded in law (such as in Massachusetts where "legality" of homosexual "marriage" has been enacted) the superior authority of God in His purpose of creating mankind female and male prevails, and should do so in the consciences of all persons recognizing the reigning force of God's will, even if revealed merely in nature, as is certainly the case with the physiological distinctions of male and female.

Add to this the judgment of the Church against sexual acts deliberately done in such a way as to prevent the possibility of conception, and at variance with the natural possibility of conception, it then follows all such same-sex acts are unchaste for they cannot be performed in true union or for children but only given to lust. Such acts insult both the personhood of humans which involves conformity to human nature and not defiance of it, and the majesty of God's purpose.

Today's attitudes and even language tend to make these natural purposes of sexual union, particularly conception of new life, as something to "protect" against, rather than welcome and embrace. American children in shockingly early education, are taught how to "protect" themselves via certain contraceptive devices. Such is called "safe sex." Sex educationists will quickly insist by that is meant protection against sexually transmitted disease. But the effect of chemical contraceptives empties that argument of any truthfulness. Thus, contraceptionists have won a victory in gaining legal approval for purchasing the "morning after" pill to "protect" from the effects of "unprotected" surrender to sexual passion the night before. It isn't disease that the "morning after" pill protects against, it is the poor baby conceived in the passion given way to, often in fornication, that is the "disease" that is eradicated.

All of these unchaste behaviors and the prevalence thereof are contributing toward diminishing marriage to a temporary situation, to a cultural or societal arrangement without any substantial perfection that makes of a man a husband and of a woman a wife.

Divorce does similar damage to the truth of marriage by making the contract, or vows, establishing a married state temporary, and no-fault divorce makes it so temporary that the very decision of a couple will end it. But the fiction of "same-sex marriage" strikes far deeper and more fatally at marriage by jettisoning from it the necessity for a cohabitating couple's being able to unite in a way that works the change to husband and wife. The availability for sexual intercourse has been from the beginning an essential for marriage. The idea of marriage of two persons lacking that capability makes "same-sex marriage" a fiction, a sham in being called one thing when in fact it is something lacking a very essential element of the genuine thing.

You can call what paralyzed persons might do football or call what someone allergic to wood might do with a rubber bat baseball — but don't expect any TV contracts. The only persons watching would be those like themselves in their disabilities. No matter how equal as humans they might be, the difference that prevents their performance on field or diamond renders them incapable of the genuine reality.

These analogies may seem farfetched and even irrational. But they are no more so than the demand of those arguing homosexuals be considered "married," without the capacity of fulfilling what is in the common – no, the unanimous – agreement of all recorded and remembered history that a marriage is the union of man and woman joining them intimately as their differences in gender makes possible primarily (though not only) for the conceiving of offspring. The right to marry has been seen as resulting from their being man and woman, not from their being two separate human beings. Remove from the reality that distinction, as some are demanding, and some jurisdictions granting, and the door is open to any arrangement for cohabitation being considered "marriage."

The traditions concerning marriage's relationship being that of husband and wife is not an arbitrary or accidental conclusion of human history. It is a natural disposal of what God proposes in His configuration of mankind as two sexes – man and woman – capable of so close an intimacy that God's revelation refers to it as becoming "one flesh." And that term in one very vital and necessary understanding refers to full, complete sexual intercourse, an immediate act, but also one ongoing when the donation of both parties unite in new human life – the conceived child. None of these unities is possible for those of identical gender, at least naturally. Technology might bring about a union of male and female elements artificially. But no technology imaginable can replace the intimacy of intercourse itself. Short of that, whatever emotion that might be exchanged by homosexuals cannot be a basis for marriage.

The full, complete giving of self to one another by man and woman is the love that Christ blessed at Cana, and the kind He meant when He compared His kingdom to a wedding feast at which all wear the proper dress or sanctity. Those things should come to our minds when we are offered the argument, "Why should those of homosexual appetites be denied what is granted to those of heterosexual ones?" The answer, of course, is that even heterosexual desires can be shameful when they are fulfilled in intentional contradiction of God's will and purposes.

If it is true that unnatural sexual appetite is in fact "natural" to some persons, then we must only conclude there is no indication from either God or nature that such desires should be succumbed to. All of us are called to a chaste life, whatever our station is. Fulfillment of lustful desires has no place in this picture. The fate of Sodom and Gomorrah would surely suggest that to surrender to such desires is a path to destruction both literally and figuratively. (There is a contrived theological speculation that sodomy didn't get its name from how sex was employed in those cities, and that their fate really came upon them because they didn't welcome strangers. If they in fact didn't welcome them, it would also imply those strangers weren't "strange" enough for the locals.)

The lack of chastity was one of the major problems that confronted St. Paul in his demands that his converts put on a new life from which the lusts of the pagans were excluded. It is becoming more and more evident that the same problems of unchastity are challenging followers of Christ in this time in history. More and more Christians seem to be surrendering to lust rather than defeating it by conformity to what Christ taught. Yet that is one sin about which Christ gave explicit directives. He told the unchaste: "Go and sin no more." It is only when we bring ourselves into conformity with these words of Christ that we will be back on the path of holiness and splendor will return to marriage as intended by Him.

Frank Morriss has been an active journalist and author since 1950. A graduate of Regis College, he holds a doctorate of law from Georgetown Univerity. Morriss taught college and founded a private Catholic school in Denver. He wrote and produced the *Divine Epic* for Catholic radio and published the material in book form. He has authored historical fiction for children as well as several books including *The Conservative Imperative, A Little Life of Our Lord, Saints in Verse*, and *Two Chapels* on John Henry Newman. A former news editor for the *Denver Catholic Register* and *National Catholic Register*, Morriss has also written for *The Wanderer* newspaper as well as served as editor of the *Forum Focus* for the Wanderer Forum Foundation.

WOMEN'S RIGHTS, LOST DIGNITY

James Bemis
Simi Valley, California

Closely bound to the Christian concept of marriage is the ideal of womanhood. The Christian wife and mother is held to be the foundation and center of the home. Pagan teaching that the woman is inferior to the man has always been especially repugnant to Catholics, who are taught early on to honor Mary, the Blessed Mother of Christ. Rather, the Church teaches that men and women are equal as persons. "Both are endowed with liberty and responsibility," Fr. E. Cahill points out in his classic *The Framework of a Christian State*, "have been redeemed by our Divine Lord, and are destined to eternal happiness."

Consequently, women have all the inalienable rights and duties as men. However, there are certain innate differences between men and women that cannot, and should not, be eliminated. This is not referring to the endowed and natural differences which make a man a man for his natural purpose and a woman a woman for hers. Rather, we are speaking here of the rights and duties which accrue to man and woman for the exercise of their separate and natural functions. For example, Catholicism teaches that when a man becomes a father, he is endowed with certain paternal rights and duties, including support and protection of the family. Similarly, when a woman becomes a mother, she receives a series of maternal duties, including the nurturing and education of her children.

The woman's role deserves a special place in society because of the duties and nature she has been given. In a properly constituted state, women's rights are safeguarded by the *illegality* of abortion and divorce. The man who tries to flee his duties as husband and father would receive no sanction from civil law, in a properly constituted state. Modern states, however, over the past decades have abandoned this exalted view of women and instead allow them to endure endless indignities and suffering at the hands of those with ill-formed consciences. Casual observation tells us the ranks of women in such a stricken state of existence are swelling with each passing year.

And the cause of this sea-change in attitude has been the women's rights movement.

As the modern world explains it, easy divorce is a key element in women's rights. We are told the equal ability and right of each spouse to end a marriage with or without just cause, to walk from their marital commitments with less complications than quitting a job, to terminate their vows leaving the dividing of assets (and sometimes children) as the only lingering complication is a wonderful thing for women and vital in freeing females from the dark, patriarchal past. This siren song has been sounded so much for so long that even women have bought into it and divorce has become the first solution to all problems in married life.

This is a lie, of course. One set of statistics debunks this notion: While the national poverty rate is 9%, it is 34% for divorced mothers. (Interestingly, it is 54% for never-married mothers, which is a related problem.) Conversely, the poverty rate for single males is 6.5% and for married couples is less than 5%. The hard-scrabble existence poverty imposes on the abandoned woman, particularly one with children, leads to further degradation. The immorality of the entire situation permeates society.

Opposed to all this is the Catholic Church, which considers protection of the sanctity of marriage one of society's fundamental obligations. Catholic social teaching defines marriage as a permanent union between a man and a woman, made under contract, for the purpose of the birth and education of children, and mutual help and companionship. The marriage contract, then, is both a social institution and a sacrament. In *European Civilization,* Fr. Jaime Balmes sums up this teaching succinctly as "one with one only, and forever."

Dignity is the state of being worthy, honored or esteemed. Its opposite is disrespect, the quality of not being considered worthy, honored or esteemed. Under Catholic canon law, such is the respect for the dignity of women that promises made to them in the sacred marriage vows cannot be shed by husbands so long as they live. As G. K. Chesterton said, "If there is such a thing as marriage, then there is no such thing as divorce."

It's hard to imagine anything more disrespectful than to be cheated upon and lied to with impunity. Yet, this is the primary outcome of the feminist movement for most women. And some women have come to use the same tactics themselves! To protect women from such indignities, the Church does not recognize the validity of divorce. Hence, in the Church's view at least, a man is expected to do the right thing: marry the mother of his children and honor his marriage vows as long as both spouses shall live.

Promiscuity is a characteristic of beasts and animals. Chastity, its opposite, is the state indicative of the more noble dignity of humans, reflecting mankind's superior intellect, consciousness and ethics, and free will. In keeping with the esteem due to each human being, the Church teaches that both men and women should live in a chaste state, according to their life's vocation. For those not married, this means abstinence from sexual activity. For married couples, fulfillment is acceptable only within the bounds of marriage. These Church teachings reflect a higher, more ennobling and dignified view of mankind (including, of course, womankind), and also helps ensure a stable, humane and orderly society. Being a communal religion, Catholicism teaches that private morality and public consequences cannot be separated.

But sadly, the teachings of the Church on this and other matters that promote a safe and ordered society, have been cast aside. And no one can say society is the better for it.

The loss of status by women explains the "why" of the statistics cited earlier, which indicate that divorced mothers are nearly seven times more likely to live in poverty than married ones, and never-married moms are nearly eleven times more frequently poor than their married counterparts. Worse, these figures deal only with the material disadvantages of abandoned women, and don't address the physical abuse and psychological torment that often comes with being degraded and deserted by one's male "companion." Most "women's rights" advocates ignore the sorry condition awaiting many female victims of divorce. Self and freedom and equal rights reign supreme.

Contrary to the popular view, then, modern females are treated with greater *dis*respect – that is, lied to, abandoned, and often treated as little more than sexual objects – than women have been traditionally, all in the name of feminism. It is difficult to see how this degradation inflicted upon modern women is superior to the Christian concept of womanhood. It would be like a butterfly wishing to become a caterpillar or a queen longing to be a charwoman. Thankfully, one force – the Catholic Church – still stands against this degradation of the woman and speaks in favor of her real human rights by honoring the sacredness of marriage and rejecting the fiction of divorce.

All the current controversies surrounding marriage (divorce laws, custody arrangements, child care payments, impact of marital breakup on children, even homosexual "marriage") have their root in our culture's deviation from the Catholic Church's teaching on the sacredness of marriage. Once society breaks from defining marriage as the Church does, as a permanent union between a man and a woman, there is no principled place to stop redefining it. Thus, the farcical notion of "gay marriage" is simply the logical consequence of the process of redefining marriage that began with allowing divorce.

Much of the blame for the loss of respect for the institution of marriage must be shouldered by the bishops in this country, who have rarely articulated and reinforced the Church's strictures on matrimony. Who can forget Cardinal Mahony celebrating a special election Mass in 1993 for the divorced mayor of Los Angeles Richard Riordan and his live-in girlfriend? One can be sure the Cardinal had little concern for the disrespect shown for Mrs. Riordan by this betrayal of the Church's teachings on the inviolability of the marital vow.

If society was truly concerned with the plight of women, it could do no better than to require men to honor the promises made to their spouses. It is a sad commentary that courts will enforce the assurances made under a business contract or even a gentleman's agreement, but not the infinitely more important ones men and women make in their marriage vows.

James Bemis is an editorial board member, weekly columnist, and film critic for *California Political Review* and his work appears regularly on the internet web site *Catholic Exchange*. He served for years as a columnist for the *Los Angeles Daily News* and his articles have appeared in several Catholic and secular publications including the *National Catholic Register, Catholic Social Science Review*, and the *Los Angeles Times*. He contributed this contemporary view of the effects of the secular culture on women over the years since the Ninth National Wanderer Forum in 1973.

CHILDREN OF THE PROMISE

Fr. Benjamin Luther
Owensboro, Kentucky

This topic is a Biblical term full of meaning for all of us in regard to marriage and the future life. I refer to the celestial nuptials awaiting all of us, the life after death, the eternal and everlasting union with Our Divine Savior in Heaven, the splendor of the final and irrevocable "marriage" or fusion of man and God in the next life.

The idea of our union with Christ in Heaven being an "espousal," a kind of marriage, is assuredly not new. The figure of marriage easily portrays the union between the human spirit — the "bride" — and Jesus Christ, the "Bridegroom." Its foundation is founded in Holy Writ. Immediately, there comes to mind the imagery of the union between Yahweh and His betrothed, or covenanted people, Israel (cf. *Osee* 2:19 *et passim*).

Jesus called Himself the "Bridegroom" (cf. *Matt.* 9:15). St. Paul picked up this theme of marriage and the spiritual life when he wrote to the Corinthian people, "For I have espoused you to one husband [i.e., Christ]" (cf. *II Cor.* 11:2). Likewise, St. John the Apostle would surely endorse our vantage point this afternoon on the analogy and relationship between the splendor of Christian marriage and the life to come. Listen to his thoughts:

> "And I saw a new heaven and a new earth. For the first heaven and the first earth was gone: and the sea is now no more. And I, John, saw the holy city, the new Jerusalem, coming down out of heaven from God, prepared as a bride adorned for her husband" (cf. *Rev.* 21:1-2).

The Apostle to the Gentile world, St. Paul, also wrote of the symbolism of the union between man and wife as referring to the intimate union between Christ and His Church (cf. *Eph.* 5:25-33) and you have already heard some splendid words on his doctrine in the talks given at this 1973 Forum. Earthly marriages, then, the glorious Sacrament of Matrimony and all that this wonderful vocation in life entails for husband, wife, and family, not to mention Church and civil society, are but a presage of the everlasting nuptials to come in that "Jerusalem on high."

Our topic reminds us, then, of our eternal vocation. We know that Heaven is essentially involved with "eternity," but in order to get some glimpse of this, we must first of all begin with where we are, that is, in "time." We are unable to step outside the here-and-now in a total manner, of course. Through the gift of Faith and the right use of reason, we are able to get some idea of the "promise" of eternal life that is ours in the "marriage" of the soul and Christ in Heaven. God, the vision of the Most Blessed Trinity, is our goal in life. God, however, is outside time. We must use our time, then, to get to Him in eternity.

The first hint of Heaven is our own restlessness in this existence of ours on planet Earth. We don't really want an endless kind of existence here. If man could invent a kind of miraculous pill or vitamin that would confer 500 years of life, there would still come a time when the experience of the weariness of life would make us want to pass from this life to an everlasting repose.

We all sense this, for no one of us here has ever been anywhere or done anything where we would be absolutely certain we would wish to spend the rest of our lives, let alone the next 500 years! So, a mere extension of time, a succession of moments, weeks, months, and years can and eventually does turn out to be a curse and not a blessing. We are not really made for Earth in a total and final manner.

We get yet another hint of the existence of Heaven in our own happiest moments. If we pause and reflect, our happiest moments partake of a kind of timelessness, a sort of glimpse of the happiness of Heaven. Artists see this in their work. Historians of the life of the immortal Mozart say he "saw" all of his musical works "at once"—a kind of *tota simul* —and only later on came the successions of moments in his musical notations. The creativity of the artist, the musician, the painter, the orator, the writer partakes of this certain timelessness. Here, we have another intimation of Heaven, our final union, our heavenly nuptials with God.

Thoughts Eternal

All of us have some intimations of immortality. There does not exist on this earth any man or woman who has reached the age of eighteen, let alone twenty-one years, who has not reflected and reflected seriously on the questions, "Why am I here? Where am I going?" Involved in these inevitable moments of introspection on the purpose of life is the question of life after death. These are graces, these are efforts on the part of the good Lord to lead men to Himself. Still, we know that many people try to immunize themselves from God, try to shut out the thought of death and eternity.

The poet T.S. Eliot gives us a few thoughts along these lines in his poem, "The Men Who Turned From God." I will give part of it here. This poem refers to a "Stranger" knocking at the door of the soul, and of course, the "Stranger" is none other than the Lord Christ.

O weariness of men who turn from God!

To the grandeur of your mind and the glory of your action,
To arts and inventions and daring enterprises,
To schemes of human greatness, thoroughly discredited.

Binding the Earth and water to your service,
Exploiting the seas and developing the mountains,
Dividing the stars into common and preferred.

Engaged in devising the perfect refrigerator,
Engaged in working out a rational morality.
Engaged in printing as many books as possible.

Plotting of happiness and flinging empty bottles,
Turning from your vacancy to fevered enthusiasm,
for nation or race or what you call, Humanity!

Though you forget the way to the Temple,
There is One who remembers the way to your door.

Life, you may evade, But death, you shall not.
You shall not deny the Stranger!

This is but another way of putting the thought of Thompson in his immortal poem, "The Hound of Heaven." Christ everlastingly pursues the soul, like a lover who seeks the beloved, desiring to consummate an unbreakable union.

Bound By Earth And Time

So, we learn some dim intimation of Heaven from our restlessness *in time*. "Our hearts are made for Thee, O God, and they are restless until they rest at last in Thee" (St. Augustine, *Confessions*). Time is the one thing that actually makes happiness an eventual impossibility – I mean total, absolute, and unalloyed happiness, inebriation in life and love and truth. We are unable, for example, because of our immersion in a succession of moments, in time, to make any sort of a "club sandwich" of the pleasures of our existence, and enjoy all of them "at once." We cannot pull past, present, and future happinesses upon one another and bathe in the delight of it all. We are very restricted beings, we humans, in so many ways.

We cannot experience the past history of our planet, except in a very circuitous manner, in a sort of vicarious way, e.g., through history books. We cannot march with Alexander in his conquests of the East, nor with Caesar in his overcoming of the West. Above all, we cannot walk and talk and live with Christ Jesus Our Lord in His earthly life in Palestine some twenty centuries ago. We cannot simultaneously enjoy the history of the civil orders of the world and also the history of the People of God in the Church!

We are so confined, we humans, so constricted by the temporal order of our existence, that we cannot, for example, enjoy winter sports in a simultaneous combination with the pleasures of a summer beach!

Time does confer enjoyments, but time also takes them away. Time, we might surmise, ought not to be such a grim guard at the door of our human existence, for time does imprison us to some extent. And yet, we have here but another hint, just from reason alone, that happiness, I mean abiding and unending happiness, exists somehow outside time, exists therefore in a certain timelessness, in an eternity.

We can see this, too, when we reflect that our happiest times were when we were oblivious of time itself — in school, in the home, at work in the office, at a musical concert, talking to a friend, reading a good book. We have all used the expression, "Time just flew by." We have here another hint of happiness unhampered by the limitations of the before-and-after, the succession of measured moments we call "time."

So, the less aware we are of time, the more we seem to be happy – surely this is a lead on how Heaven must be! Heaven must be outside of time where we can reach out and grasp and enjoy all happiness in one, full moment!

And so, we have the "conditions" of happiness. We are still here, however, we are still earthbound pilgrims wending our way to celestial nuptials, the final marital union of the supernatural order in that "splendor of Christian marriage" we call sanctifying grace.

Our wish for one another is, "Go to Heaven." Let us not think of Heaven as being "out there." Perhaps all of us tend to picture Heaven as outside of ourselves. This can be a dangerous tendency, for if we picture Heaven as being at the end of time, then we tend to postpone making final decisions, decisions to commit ourselves to the Lord Jesus Christ, once and for all.

No, Heaven is not "out there," but rather, "in here." In like manner, by the same token, Hell is not "down there," but also "in here." We are already in Heaven, or in Hell, in this life, depending on whether or not we are in God's grace!

Haven't we all seen Heaven in the faces of others? Who has not seen a bit of Heaven in the face of a child? Who has not come across something of Heaven in the face of an elderly person who has lived a long and godly life? Don't we see some suggestion of Heaven on the faces of brides and grooms at the nuptial Mass? Have we not one and all encountered saintly priests, Religious, and lay people who give a certain aura of evidence that they bear Heaven within them, that they are God-bearers! Heaven can be reflected in the faces of all these people – Why? – because Love is within them, and St. John says, "God is Love." Yes, we have all encountered these saintly persons who had what one writer called "... an imprisoned loveliness obtaining outward utterance" in face and action.

No, Heaven is not "out there." Heaven is within and is related to a good and holy life as the seed is related to the fully grown plant. Heaven is not related to a good life as reward is related to a contest – for example, a trophy to a race or a gold medal to study, for these things need not follow one another. A trophy is extrinsic to the nature of a race. Heaven is better pictured as knowledge related to study — surely, knowledge follows upon study as from a necessity. It is intrinsic, not extrinsic.

In like manner, eternal damnation is not related to a bad life as spanking is related to an act of disobedience. One need not follow the other — in our modern times, indeed, it seems that they do not follow one another often enough! Rather, Hell follows an evil life as corruption of the flesh follows upon death. There is an intrinsic relationship.

So, we have Heaven within us, the seed of glory growing and growing and blooming forth from day to day and year to year. This seed of glory, this Heaven "in here" is sanctifying grace, our created share in the uncreated Grace we call God. Because of Baptism, we can share in Heaven, beginning on this Earth. Heaven is not far off, it begins here, we get faint glimpses of it here, and it will unfold in a never-passing moment someday, when we step from this life into Heaven, or from Purgatory into the Beatific Vision of the Father, the Son, and the Holy Spirit.

On the night of His Last Supper, Christ washed the feet of His disciples, and by this example and His words, set an example of utter forgetfulness of self. This is dramatically realized when we come to think that He was up against His Passion in a matter of moments. He knew He was facing death, the ugly betrayal of Judas, the denial of Peter, and He knew all of these things with the utmost clarity, as Christ was God. In the face of all these things, you might think that Our Lord would think a little of Himself, but no; His thoughts are seen to be of His disciples, and also of us. "Let not your heart be troubled" "I go to prepare a place for you" "In my Father's house are many mansions" (*John* 14:1-2). He promised to send the Comforter. God prepares for our eternal good with infinite care and exceeding preparation, and He notes that He has prepared a place for each one of us as an individual person. We might say that the thoughtfulness of Our Blessed Savior in regard to each one of us is truly astounding. It boggles the imagination!

Yes, indeed, we are all moving toward nuptials, toward heavenly nuptials, toward the final marriage between the soul and God the Blessed Three, the ultimate meaning of the "Splendor of Christian Marriage." We will all reunite in that wedding feast – parted husbands and wives, parents and children, friends and neighbors – there is another hint here of the existence of Heaven in the fact that two hearts grow together and there is pain in the parting of death and we refuse to believe that this severance in love is final.

On Our Way to the Final Marriage

We are on our way to nuptials! Just go back into your own life and conjure up your greatest moments of happiness in the thrill of living, go back to some great ecstasy of love, to some intuition of truth, to some glimpse of goodness, to some great day in your life. Now, if we could raise all of these things to a focal point, as a magnifying glass draws together and fuses into one the rays of the sun, if we could concentrate all happiness in our life into one such point, we would have some very dim suggestion of Heaven — perfect Life, perfect Truth, perfect Love.

We are on our way to nuptials, celestial nuptials, a heavenly marriage, an unbreakable union with God and one another in Christ in the mansions of Heaven.

What a glorious destiny is ours – sons and daughters, children all, of the promise of God – ours, and for free, because we have been gifted with the Catholic Faith and given a share in the Divine life!

When we arrive at our heavenly nuptials, there will be some surprises. Some will be there whom we thought would not make it. Some will not be there, and we thought they would be.

You know what I am going to say in conclusion: The greatest surprise of all will be to find that you, and I, are there, in Heaven, safe in the arms of Our Father, forever! God grant us all this gift of the heavenly marriage in the Jerusalem above!

Fr. Benjamin Luther delivered this homily at the concluding Mass of the Ninth National Wanderer Forum. Father Luther has directed many operations for the Diocese of Owensboro, as well as serving as pastor at several parishes in the years since the Forum. He is currently working in a parish and with the Marian Shrine in Bowling Green, Kentucky.

In Retrospect...

"Where will the 'alternatives' to the family end?" the headline asked this spring of 2007. In reading the words of the 1973 Wanderer Forum speakers, it is plain that so much has changed and yet nothing really has.

• Over 35,000,000 million abortions have taken place since the anger of 1973 and the need for a constitutional amendment recognizing the personhood of the unborn child still remains, although the anti-life arsenal now includes over-the-counter pills to flush out the new child at home.

• Nearly half of the marriages contracted now end in divorce. Where has the concept of sacrificial love – agape – gone, if it had ever been taught in the first place. Meanwhile the same-sex activities whispered about a generation ago have been flaunted openly and defiantly, even before the Eucharist in the cathedrals across the land.

• And women didn't need an Equal Rights Amendment after all. The upheaval of values in society brought women into the workplace to achieve better lifestyles and children first to daycare and then to home-alone status. Without the mother in the home, the children have come of age answering to no one for their deeds, mannerless, faithless, and undisciplined.

But there is hope, little glimmers of light within the human heart yearning for something better, for something good and pure and idealistic under the ugly layers of today's secular culture. Pope John Paul II recognized this and called those who believe to a new missionary objective: to revolutionize society in a spiritual way, by recalling people to the realities of God, Christianity, and of the Church.

It can be done, person by person, marriage by marriage, family by family through prayer and the grace of God. We need only the courage to begin.

– The Editor